Forgetting the Root

The Emergence of Christianity from Judaism

Terrance Callan

PAULIST PRESS
New York/Mahwah

Biblical quotations in this book are from the *Revised Standard Version*.

Maps by *Frank Sabatté, C.S.P.*

Library of Congress
Catalog Card Number: 85-62929

ISBN: 0-8091-2778-4

Published by Paulist Press
997 Macarthur Boulevard
Mahwah, New Jersey 07430

Printed and bound in the
United States of America

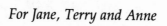

For Jane, Terry and Anne

CONTENTS

Now I am speaking to you Gentiles . . . . If some of the branches were broken off, and you, a wild olive shoot, were grafted in their place to share the richness of the olive tree, do not boast over the branches. If you do boast, remember it is not you that support the root, but the root that supports you. You will say, "Branches were broken off so that I might be grafted in." That is true. They were broken off because of their unbelief, but you stand fast only through faith. So do not become proud, but stand in awe. For if God did not spare the natural branches, neither will he spare you. Note then the kindness and the severity of God; severity toward those who have fallen, but God's kindness to you, provided you continue in his kindness, otherwise you too will be cut off. And even the others, if they do not persist in their unbelief, will be grafted in, for God has power to graft them in again. For if you have been cut from what is by nature a wild olive tree, and grafted, contrary to nature, into a cultivated olive tree, how much more will these natural branches be grafted back into their own olive tree.

Romans 11:13, 17–24

INTRODUCTION

Scholars in the field of Christian origins are well aware of the intimate relationship between Judaism and Christianity during the first centuries of the latter's existence. One such scholar, Samuel Sandmel, has even said that Pharisaic Judaism and Christianity are the two forms in which Judaism enters the Common Era. However, most twentieth century Jews and Christians are not equally well aware of this intimate relationship; they tend to project the contemporary relationship between Judaism and Christianity back onto the first centuries of the Common Era. It is chiefly for their benefit that the following pages describe the emergence of Christianity from Judaism, showing how the present relationship between the two came into being. I will trace this development as far as the fourth century CE because it was essentially complete at that time. I hope that this will be of historical interest and, even more, that it may open up new possibilities for the contemporary relationship between Judaism and Christianity.

While scholars agree that Judaism and Christianity are intimately related, there is presently considerable discussion about the exact nature of that relationship. The catalyst for this discussion was Rosemary Radford Ruether's claim in *Faith and Fratricide* that Christianity is intrinsically anti-Jewish. This thesis has stimulated many to modify or reject it. A collection of such responses is found in *Anti-Semitism and the Foundations of Christianity*, edited by Alan T. Davies. To date, the most substantial response to Ruether is that of John Gager in *The Origins of Anti-Semitism*. Gager has argued that at least the apostle Paul was

1

not at all anti-Jewish, and that competition between Christians and Jews for converts and for the favor of pagans was a major factor in the development of Christian anti-Judaism.

Though I will not speak directly to the question of the origins of anti-Semitism, my description of the gradual emergence of Christianity from Judaism will imply modification of Ruether's thesis. It will first of all show that Christianity was not anti-Jewish from the beginning; and secondly it will show that the way in which Christianity became separate from Judaism was itself an important factor in the development of Christian anti-Jewish views.

In a certain sense Christianity emerged from Judaism as a separate religion because Jesus appeared and was accepted by some Jews as the promised messiah. If Jesus had never appeared, or if all Jews had become his followers (or none did), no separation could have occurred. However, this separation also depended on additional factors which I will describe. I will focus on two such factors: first, the church's decision that Gentile Christians need not keep the Jewish law; and second, the eventual decline of Jewish membership in the church.

Briefly, I will argue:

(a) that Jesus did not separate himself from Judaism, but addressed the Judaism of his day in a prophetic manner;

(b) that the earliest church, in its belief that Jesus was the messiah, was a sect within Judaism but not separate from it;

(c) that the adoption of a liberal policy toward Gentile converts by the greater part of the early church was the decisive factor which separated it from Judaism;

(d) that those who had a more conservative policy toward Gentile converts remained closely connected with Judaism until developments within Judaism separated them;

(e) that the liberal branch of the church was first composed of Jewish Christians who retained a positive view of Judaism despite holding that Gentile Christians were not bound by the law; and

(f) that eventually the liberal branch of the church was composed entirely of Gentiles who developed a negative view of Jewish Christianity and Judaism; at this point the separation of Christianity from Judaism was complete and Christianity became anti-Jewish.

I will make considerable use of the terms 'conservative' and 'liberal.' I will use 'conservative' to describe Christians who held the view that Gentile Christians must keep the Jewish law, i.e., become Jews. I will use 'liberal' to describe Christians holding the view that Gentile Christians need not keep the Jewish law.

We could distinguish between conservative Jewish and conservative Gentile Christians, i.e., between those who believed that Gentile Christians must keep the Jewish law who were Jews before they became Christians, and those holding this belief who kept the law only after becoming Christians. The term 'Jewish Christian' often designates the former, and 'Judaizer' the latter. I will not make use of this terminology because it obscures what I consider the crucial fact that there were both conservative and liberal Jewish Christians. Since both conservative Jewish and conservative Gentile Christians kept the law as Christians, and so in some sense were Jews, I will speak simply of conservative Jewish Christians.

The case is entirely different with respect to liberal Christians, however. Here we must distinguish carefully between liberal Jewish and liberal Gentile Christians. Although both agreed that Gentiles need not keep the law, the earliest liberal Jewish Christians themselves did keep the law. Thus even though they considered that keeping the law was not necessary for salvation, and so took a very different view of it than did non-Christian Jews, they retained a positive appreciation of the law, or at least of Judaism. Therefore, liberal Jewish Christians almost necessarily saw a very close connection between Judaism and Christianity and consequently were not anti-Jewish, though they were critical of non-Christian Jews. However, liberal Gentile Christians easily lost this positive appreciation of the law and Judaism, and understood the arguments against Gentile observance of the law more absolutely than Jewish Christians did. The conservative branch of the church never seems to have been equal in numbers or influence to the liberal branch of the church. Thus the story of the final separation of Christianity from Judaism is the story of how liberal Jewish Christian domination of the church gave way to liberal Gentile Christian domination. When this development was complete, even Jewish converts to liberal Christianity abandoned observance of the law. Therefore, the distinction between liberal Jewish and liberal Gentile Christians is significant mainly during the early centuries of the church's existence.

From all of this it is clear that the attitude of Christians to the Jewish law was a key factor in the relationship of Christianity to Judaism. As long as Christians observed the law, they remained in union with Judaism. The decision that Gentile Christians need not keep the law began the separation of Christianity from Judaism. This separation was complete when liberal Gentile Christians developed a negative view of the law and Judaism itself. Of course, with the exception of Marcion and the Gnostics, Christians did not go so far in rejecting the law that they rejected the Hebrew scriptures themselves; for most Christians these writings retained value, principally as predictions of Jesus. Because of this there is an ambivalence in the attitude of most Christians toward the law, an ambivalence not fully resolved even today.

After tracing in greater detail the development I have outlined here, I will conclude my discussion with some observations on the retrieval of some of the positions discussed for the present day. The past may offer some helpful clues to a better relationship between Christianity and Judaism in the present.

A survey of this sort passes over a multitude of disputable matters in silence. However, except where otherwise noted, the views I present are supported by a substantial body of scholarly opinion, at least partly indicated in the bibliography. The bibliography includes those books and articles which are mentioned by name in the text, as well as those which underlie the discussion in the text. However, the overall reconstruction of early Christian history which I present here is my own.

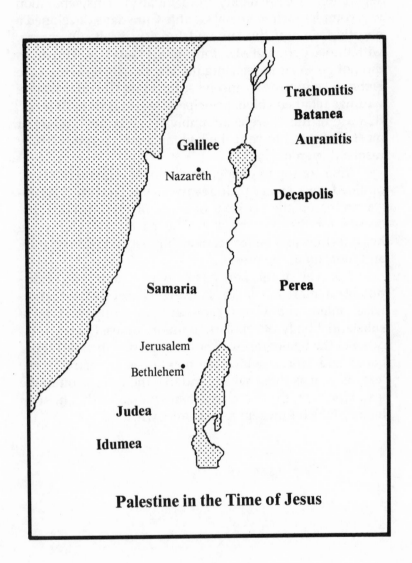

Palestine in the Time of Jesus

I.

JESUS

That Jesus did not separate himself from Judaism, but addressed the Judaism of his day in a prophetic manner.

Introduction

In thinking about Jesus we tend to view him as the founder of Christianity, a new religion which replaced Judaism, at least for its adherents. And in the sense that Jesus initiated this historical development, we are quite right to do so. However, if we look at Jesus without this historical perspective, the picture is somewhat different. Then it appears that Jesus is best understood within the framework of the Judaism of his day.

At the time of Jesus the Jewish people were scattered throughout the world, much as they are today. Jesus lived in Palestine, the homeland of the Jews. According to the earliest accounts of his birth (Matt 1–2; Luke 1–2), Jesus was born in Bethlehem in Judea during the reign of Herod the Great (Matt 2:1; Luke 1:5; 2:1–7). Since Herod died in 4 BCE, this would be the latest date possible for the birth of Jesus. Jesus' public life, which lasted one to three years, began in about 29 CE according to Luke (Luke 3:1). According

7

to the gospels, Jesus was active mainly in Galilee and Judea, but also in the area to the north of Galilee, as well as the Decapolis, Samaria and Perea.

All of this territory had been under Roman control since 63 BCE. From 37 to 4 BCE most of it was ruled by Herod the Great as a client king. On his death Herod's three sons inherited his kingdom. Archelaus became ethnarch of Idumea, Judea and Samaria; Herod Antipas became tetrarch of Galilee and Perea; and Philip became tetrarch of Batanea, Trachonitis and Auranitis. The latter two retained control of their territory during the public ministry of Jesus. However, the first of a series of Roman governors replaced Archelaus in 6 CE. Pontius Pilate was the Roman governor of Idumea, Judea and Samaria from 26 to 36 CE.

Roman rule was not popular in Palestine. The Romans offended the religious sensibilities of the Jews in many ways, often without intending to do so. Roman rule brought opportunities for some to become rich and made many poor. Those who benefited from their rule, e.g., the Sadducees, the priestly aristocracy of Israel, collaborated with the Romans in ruling the country. Others resisted the Romans in various ways. The Pharisees tried to ignore the Romans. The Zealots sought to overthrow Roman rule militarily; this desire eventually issued in rebellion in 66 CE. The Essenes withdrew from the larger community to hold themselves in readiness for God's intervention to save them. John the Baptist and Jesus called upon the Jewish people to reform their lives in preparation for such an intervention of God. Even if it was not in itself rebellious, it was always possible for a popular movement to lead to an outbreak of hostility to the Roman rule. The execution of Jesus was probably an attempt to prevent such an outbreak of hostility.

Our information about first century Palestine comes mainly from two works of the Jewish historian Josephus (c. 37–100): his account of the *Jewish War* and the parallel to it in the later sections of his *Jewish Antiquities*.

Our information about Jesus comes mainly from the gospels of Matthew, Mark, Luke and John. As is well-known, it is difficult to recover the facts of Jesus' career. This is so principally because those who first wrote the story of Jesus already interpreted it from the perspective of their own situation, just as we do. Here we will not be able to make a serious attempt to recover the historical Jesus. But a review of certain aspects of Jesus' career, aspects on which most of the New Testament witnesses agree and which are probably historical, supports the contention that Jesus did not break completely with Judaism, but remained within its compass. However, we will also see in Jesus anticipations of that which later separated the church from Judaism, i.e., inclusion of Gentiles and a new interpretation of the Mosaic law.

The Jewishness of Jesus

In their accounts of his birth Matthew and Luke emphasize the Jewish origins of Jesus; Luke mentions explicitly that Jesus was circumcised on the eighth day (Luke 2:21) and details other instances of his parents' fidelity to the law (2:22–40). This picture of Jesus' early life serves the special interests of Matthew and Luke, which we will discuss below. However, it is confirmed by the presentation of Jesus, common to all four gospels, as being frequently in the synagogues

Mark 1:21–23/Luke 4:33; Mark 1:39/Matt 4:23/Luke 4:44;

Mark 3:1/Matt 12:9/Luke 6:6; Mark 6:2/Matt 13:54/Luke 4:16; Matt 9:35; Luke 4:15; 13:10; John 6:59; 18:20

or the temple

Mark 11:15–19/Matt 21:12–13/Luke 19:45–46/John 2:13–17; Mark 11:27/Matt 21:23/Luke 20:1; Mark 12:35; 13:1/Matt 24:1; Mark 14:49/Matt 26:55/Luke 22:53/John 18:20; Matt 21:14–15; Luke 19:47; 21:37–38; John 8:2; 5:14; 7:14, 28: 8:20; 10:23

and as observing various feasts: passover (Mark 14:12–16/ Matt 26:17–20/Luke 22:7–15; John 2:13, 23), tabernacles (John 7:2, 10), dedication (John 10:22?) and an unnamed feast (John 5:1). This indicates both Jesus' own Jewishness and the focus of his ministry on Israel.

Jesus' Ministry to Israel

The Jewishness of Jesus' closest associates—the Twelve—also indicates the focus of his ministry on Israel. Among other things their names reveal their Jewishness (Mark 3:16–19/Matt 10:2–4/Luke 6:14–16/Acts 1:13). It is striking, however, that two of them—Andrew and Philip—have Greek names, and that one—Bartholomew—has a name which may show Greek influence, i.e., Bartholomew = bar Tholmai = Ptolemy. This may simply reflect the impact of Greek culture on Palestine generally, or suggest that Jesus' followers came in part from circles especially subject to that impact.

The gospels present Jesus as having fairly frequent contact with Gentiles, or at least those from Gentile territory, either because they come to him (Mark 3:7–8/Matt

4:25/Luke 6:17) or because he goes to them (Mark 5:1–20/ Matt 8:28–34/Luke 8:26–39; Matt 8:5–13/Luke 7:1–10/John 4:46–54; Mark 7:31–37; 8:22–26). That this is exceptional, however, is clear from Jesus' response to the Syro-Phoenician woman's request for the healing of her daughter, 'It is not right to take the children's bread and throw it to the dogs' (Mark 7:24–30/Matt 15:21–28). According to Matthew Jesus first says that he was sent only to the lost sheep of the house of Israel (15:24). Matthew also says that Jesus explicitly prohibited his associates from mission among the Gentiles (10:5–6). This probably reflects Matthew's special interests, but is in accord with the picture of Jesus' activities in the gospels generally.

Jewish Reaction to Jesus

According to the gospels Jesus met with wide popular acceptance by the people of Israel. This is clear in such incidents as Jesus' miraculous feeding of five thousand (Mark 6:32–44/Matt 14:13–21/Luke 9:10–17/John 6:1–15) and his triumphal entry into Jerusalem (Mark 11:1–10/Matt 21:1–9/Luke 19:28–40/John 12:12–19). Of course, we do not know the exact nature of this acceptance; it probably ranged from mere curiosity to serious commitment. On the other hand, those near him rejected Jesus (Mark 3:21), as did his own country, i.e., the town of Nazareth (Mark 6:1–6/Matt 13:53–58/Luke 4:16–30), and especially the leaders of the people, variously specified as scribes, Pharisees, chief priests, Herodians, Sadducees, elders, etc. The gospel of John portrays Jesus in frequent conflict with 'the Jews,' but this is certainly anachronistic, reflecting the circumstances in which John was written rather than those of Jesus' day. The combination of popular acceptance with rejection by the leaders of the people appears especially clear in notices that the leaders were afraid to move against Jesus because of his popularity (Mark 12:12/Matt 21:46/Luke 20:19; 19:47–48), that they feared his popularity (Mark 11:18; John 11:45–53) and that they incited the people against Jesus (Mark 15:11/Matt 27:20).

Jesus and the Law

The most common reason for conflict between Jesus and the leaders of the people was Jesus' interpretation of the law. He defended his disciples when they plucked grain and ate it on the sabbath (Mark 2:23–28/Matt 12:1–8/Luke 6:1–5) and defended himself for healing on the sabbath (Mark 3:1–6/Matt 12:9–14/Luke 6:6–11; 13:10–17; 14:1–6; John 5:1–10; 7:21–4; 9:1–16). He defended his disciples for eating with unwashed hands (Mark 7:1–23/Matt 15:1–20). He argued against divorce (Mark 10:2–9/Matt 19:3–12; 5:31–32), and he defended himself for eating and associating with sinners (Mark 2:15–17/Matt 9:10–13/Luke 5:29–32; Matt 11:19/Luke 7:34; 7:36–50; 15:1–2; 19:1–10) and his disciples for not fasting (Mark 2:18–22/Matt 9:14–17/Luke 5:33–39). The evangelists handled these issues differently, according to the way each saw the relationship between Christianity and Judaism. But in no case did Jesus simply reject the law. Rather, he proposed an interpretation of it which was disputable, and thus implicitly affirmed it in some measure.

Parallels between Jesus' critical statements about the law and statements made by other Jews lend support to this view. For example, part of Jesus' defense of his disciples for plucking and eating grain on the sabbath is the statement that the sabbath was made for human beings, not human beings for the sabbath (Mark 2:27). This is very similar to the statement found in the Mekilta, the rabbinic commentary on Exodus, that the sabbath is surrendered to you (i.e., human beings), but you are not surrendered to the sabbath (Mekilta, Shabbata 1.27–8). Similarly Jesus defended his disciples for eating with unwashed hands by saying that nothing outside someone can, by going into that person, defile; but that which comes out of someone is what defiles (Mark 7:15/Matt 15:11). Pesikta Rabbati, a collection of rabbinic homilies for various feasts, attributes a somewhat similar statement to Rabbi Johanan ben Zakkai. He said that contact with a dead person does not defile, nor does water cleanse from this defilement, but that it is necessary to observe the laws on these matters because they were given by God (Pesikta Rabbati 40b).

Jesus' argument against divorce has a rather striking parallel in the Dead Sea Scrolls, writings of the Essenes. Jesus argued against divorce by appealing to Genesis 1:27, and the Essene argument against divorce in the Damascus Document also appeals to this text (CD 4:20–21). Here and in another reference to the prohibition of divorce in the Temple Scroll (11 Q Temple 57:17–19), the Essene writers are also relying on an interpretation of Leviticus 18:18; consequently they do not seem to regard their anti-divorce position as controversial. Jesus clearly does consider his position on divorce controversial in Mark 10:2–9/Matt 19:3–12; 5:31–32. However, Luke does not seem to regard Jesus' teaching against divorce as controversial (16:16–18) and may presuppose something like the Essene interpretation of Leviticus 18:18. Angelo Tosato has recently argued that this interpretation preserves the original meaning of the passage.

Jesus' affirmation of the law is explicit in the synoptic gospels (cf. also Gal 4:4). They report that Jesus affirmed the ten commandments (Mark 10:17–22/Matt 19:16–22/ Luke 18:18–23), the two great commandments, i.e., Deut 6:4 and Lev 19:18 (Mark 12:28–34/Matt 22:34–40/Luke 10:25–28; cf. John 13:34; 15:12), and even the smallest items of the law (Matt 5:17–20/Luke 16:16–17). Jesus sent the leper he had cleansed to the priest so that he might offer the sacrifice which Moses commanded (Mark 1:40–45/Matt 8:1–4/Luke 5:12–14). He affirmed the tithing of spices (Matt 23:23/Luke 11:42). Matthew reports that Jesus paid the temple tax (17:24–27).

In addition to defending his interpretation of the law, Jesus also attacked those who criticized it. He accused them of hypocrisy (Mark 7:1–23/Matt 15:1–20; Mark 12:38–40/Matt 23/Luke 20:45–47 and 11:37–54) and, in a parable, of being wicked overseers (Mark 12:1–12/Matt 21:33–46/ Luke 20:9–19). John records even more severe criticism of 'the Jews' who oppose Jesus (cf. 8:31–47).

Jesus' Claims About Himself

Another source of conflict between Jesus and the leaders of the people of Israel was what Jesus claimed about himself. The gospels record that he gave offense by saying that he could forgive sins (Mark 2:1–12/Matt 9:1–8/Luke 5:17–26; 7:48–50). In Jesus' time illness and suffering were seen as a consequence of sin (cf. Luke 13:1–5; John 9:1–2), and Jesus' claim to be able to forgive sins may be an explication of what is implicit in his power to heal. Jesus' admission at his trial that he was the messiah, the son of God, was also held against him (Mark 14:55–65/Matt 26:59–68/ Luke 22:66–71; cf. John 19:7). John records other occasions when the relationship which Jesus claimed to have with God was seen as offensive (cf. 5:17–18, 10:31–39).

The Condemnation of Jesus

However, despite the impression which the gospels convey, the hostility of the leaders of Israel probably did not derive principally from their concern over his interpretation of the law or his claims about himself. It seems most likely that they feared he would incite rebellion against Rome, as John says explicitly (11:45–53; cf. Mark 11:18). This seems to have been the ground on which Pilate condemned him (Mark 15:2–5/Matt 27:11–14/Luke 23:2–5/John 18:29–38; 19:12–16; Mark 15:26/Matt 27:37/Luke 23:38/John 19:19–22).

Summary

Jesus was a Jew, and his ministry was directed mainly to Jews, though he had some contact with Gentiles. He was very popular with the Jewish people in general, but not with their leaders. The leaders rejected him because his interpretation of the law differed from theirs and because of what he claimed about himself, but above all because he seemed likely to upset the status quo and cause trouble with Rome. Jesus seems to fit easily the pattern of the prophet within Israel, challenging accepted ways of doing things and so meeting with resistance. Though he himself was no more separate from Israel than any of the prophets, his contacts with Gentiles and his special interpretation of the law anticipate the factors which later separated the church from Israel.

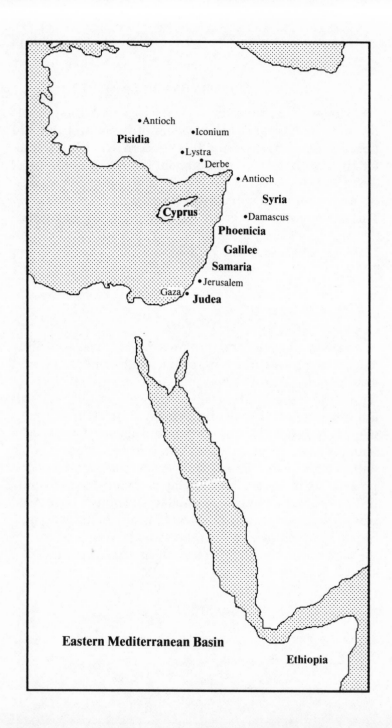

Eastern Mediterranean Basin

II.

THE EARLY CHURCH

Introduction

For our purposes the period of the early church extends from the death and resurrection of Jesus (c. 30–32 CE) to the so-called 'Apostolic Council' in about 48 CE. During this time the early church spread from Jerusalem (and perhaps Galilee) to Samaria (Acts 8:4–25), Ethiopia (Acts 8:26–39), Damascus (cf. Acts 9:2), the towns of Judea (Acts 8:40; 9:32–10:48), Phoenicia, Cyprus and Antioch (Acts 11:19). From Antioch a missionary expedition spread the church to the cities of Asia Minor principally Pisidian Antioch, Iconium, Lystra and Derbe (Acts 13–14).

All of this territory lay within the Roman empire, headed successively by the emperors Tiberius (14–37 CE), Caligula (37–41) and Claudius (41–54). All was relatively stable politically except for Palestine. From 41–44 CE Herod Agrippa I ruled as king over the reunited kingdom of his grandfather Herod the Great. After his death a series of Roman procurators ruled Palestine; under their administrations the revolution of 66 CE grew closer and closer.

The most important consequence of the geographical spread of the church was the inclusion of large numbers of Gentiles within it. There were many Gentiles in Palestine, and very likely some of them became Christians. Likewise, there were many Jews outside of Palestine, and it seems likely that the church spread first among them. But the spread of the church outside of Palestine also led to its growth among the Gentiles. And this insured that the attitude taken toward Gentile converts became an important matter for the church.

Our information about Palestine during the period of the early church comes chiefly from Josephus. We know about the Roman empire as a whole during this time from the writings of two historians: Tacitus (c. 55–120), whose *Annals* covers the reigns of the emperors from Tiberius to Nero, and Suetonius (69–140), whose *Lives of the Caesars* discusses the emperors from Julius Caesar to Domitian.

Our chief source of information about the early church itself is the Acts of the Apostles, the continuation of the gospel of Luke. According to Acts the church was first established in Jerusalem and spread out from there in a fairly orderly fashion. However, there is reason to believe that Luke has simplified things somewhat. For one thing, he omits any reference to resurrection appearances of Jesus in Galilee (see Mark 16:7; Matt 28:16–20; John 21); such appearances may well have been connected with the beginning of a branch of the church in Galilee at the same time that the Jerusalem church came into being. And another indication that Luke has simplified his picture is that he tells us that Paul intends to persecute Christians in Damascus (Acts 9:1–2) without telling us how there came to be Christians in Damascus. Likewise, when Paul arrived in Rome, he found Christians there (Acts 28:15), and earlier he had written them a letter. Luke says nothing about the spread of Christianity to Rome. Thus it seems that the early history of the church may be somewhat more complex than we might guess from the account in Acts.

That the earliest church, in its belief that Jesus was the messiah, was a sect within Judaism, but not separate from it.

The Earliest Church and Judaism

Contrary to what we might expect, it does not seem that belief in Jesus in itself separated the early church from Judaism completely, though the development of Christology later played a part in this separation. Judaism has usually been more tolerant of divergent beliefs than of divergent behavior. Because of this, the belief that Jesus was the messiah did not separate Christians from Judaism, though it did set them apart within Judaism. The early church was not separate from Judaism until it began to deviate from adherence to the Jewish law.

The earliest Christian church came into being among those followers of Jesus who, because of his resurrection, believed that he was the messiah. Jesus himself had apparently not laid great stress on a claim to be the messiah. And after his crucifixion he certainly bore no striking resemblance to the messiah of contemporary Jewish expectation. Consequently, it is difficult to understand why the earliest church affirmed that he was the messiah.

The best explanation seems to be that proposed by Nils A. Dahl: precisely because Pilate crucified Jesus as king of the Jews (Mark 15:26/Matt 27:37/Luke 23:38/John 19:19–22), i.e., messianic pretender, his resurrection was perceived as God's vindication of him, and equivalently a declaration that he was truly the messiah. Because his followers' faith that he was the messiah arose in this way, they were able to reformulate the idea of the messiah to fit the facts of Jesus' career, having as a secure starting point God's own assurance that Jesus was the messiah. They did this principally by searching the Hebrew scriptures for prophecies of the events of Jesus' life and especially his death and resurrection. And they found a substantial quantity of such prophecies.

Although their belief that Jesus was the messiah, and even more a crucified messiah, set the earliest church apart from the rest of Judaism, the early Christians continued to be Jews. The portrait of the earliest church in Acts emphasizes its Jewish piety, referring several times to the early Christians' presence in the temple (Acts 2:46; 3:1; 5:12). This suits Luke's theological outlook, as we will see, but probably is also an accurate reflection of the Jewishness of the early church. At its beginning, the early church can probably best be seen as a sect within Judaism.

We can see from other messianic movements within Judaism that the belief in some person as the messiah, even when that involved reinterpretation of what it meant to be the messiah, led to the formation of a Jewish sect, not a separate religion. Separation was the result of failing to adhere to the Jewish law, not of any doctrinal peculiarity in itself.

The Sabbatian Movement

This is clearest in the case of the messianic movement centered around Sabbatai Zevi beginning in the seventeenth century, which has been described by Gershom Scholem. With the support of Nathan of Gaza, in 1665 Sabbatai Zevi proclaimed himself the messiah. In 1666 Sabbatai Zevi was forced to apostatize, becoming a Muslim. But his followers adjusted their ideas about the messiah to accommodate this, much as the followers of Jesus had earlier reformulated the idea of the messiah to accommodate the crucifixion of Jesus. And like early Christianity, the Sabbatian movement was at first a sect within Judaism. It became heretical when accepting Sabbatai Zevi as messiah led to antinomian behavior on the part of his followers. The chief exponent of such antinomianism was Jacob Frank (1726–1791). Christianity and the Sabbatian movement are different in many ways. But they resemble one another in being messianic movements and in requiring substantial reinterpretation of what it means to be messiah, both of which made them sects within Judaism.

That the adoption of a liberal policy toward Gentile converts by the greater part of the early church was the decisive factor which separated it from Judaism.

Admission of Gentiles into the Church

If the belief that Jesus was the messiah did not separate the early church from Judaism completely, then the cause of that complete separation remains to be identified. I suggest that this cause was the decision, made very early in the history of the church, to admit Gentiles to membership in the church without requiring that they keep the Jewish law.

According to Acts the first Gentile convert to Christianity was Cornelius, who was converted at the preaching of Peter. When the Holy Spirit fell upon Cornelius and his household, just as it had upon Peter and the other followers of Jesus at Pentecost, Peter concluded that they could be baptized (Acts 10:44–48; 11:15–18). Later this was part of the basis for an official decision that circumcision, i.e., conversion to Judaism, was not necessary for Gentile converts to Christianity. This decision was made at the so-called 'Apostolic Council' in 48 CE (Acts 15:1–35).

Even if the details of Luke's account are questionable, it is entirely likely that the first Gentiles became Christians in the manner he describes. It seems quite probable that Gentiles first became Christians when they received the Holy Spirit after listening to Christian preaching (cf. Gal 3:1–5). But, as Luke does not make clear, two different conclusions were possible. One could say that the Gentiles, even though they had received the Spirit as Gentiles, were obliged to become Jews and keep the Jewish law. And this might be the more natural view for the early church to take, in view of the Jewish understanding of the origin and purpose of the law. Or one could say, as Peter does in Luke's story, that the gift of the Spirit to uncircumcised Gentiles showed that circumcision was not necessary for them. The first approach we might call 'conservative,' and the second 'liberal.' According to Luke, at the beginning the whole church was conservative (at least implicitly), and later under the influence of Peter's experience with Cornelius and the discussion at the Apostolic Council, the whole church became liberal.

This is the result of considerable simplification. While it is probably true that the most important leaders of the early church embraced the liberal position at the Apostolic Council (as Paul's very different account of this meeting in Gal 2:1–10 confirms), it is clear that there continued to be conservative Christians long after the Council; and it seems likely that there were liberal Christians before Peter baptized Cornelius.

If the earlier existence of a liberal group within the church surfaces anywhere in Acts, it is in what Luke says about Stephen and his associates, the Hellenists. Luke does not present them as liberal Christians, but there are good reasons for thinking that they may have been such, and that the accusation against them which Luke calls false was actually true (Acts 6:14). First, it seems clear from Luke's presentation (though he does not say this explicitly) that Stephen and the Hellenists differed from the rest of the early Christians theologically. This seems to follow from the fact that non-Christian Jews persecuted the Hellenists, but not the apostles (and presumably the other non-Hellenist Christians) (Acts 8:1). However, it is difficult to see what the theological difference is. One possibility which lies close to hand is that the Hellenists had a liberal policy toward Gentile converts. Acts 11:19–20 reports that some of them preached Jesus to the Greeks in Antioch, converting many. It is tempting to assume that this evangelization of Gentiles occurred earlier than the text of Acts suggests (possibly in Damascus), and that it was the reason for the persecution of the Hellenists. They would have posed a threat to Judaism which the conservative Jewish Christians did not. Luke may have de-emphasized the liberalism of the Hellenists in an effort to connect the beginning of the liberal mission to the Gentiles with the figure of Peter, whose prestige would lend support to such a mission.

The career of Paul provides an additional indication of the early existence of a liberal group within the early church (the Hellenists or some other). Paul became a Christian only a few years after the crucifixion and resurrection of Jesus, and before that he was a persecutor of Christians. The motives for his persecution are obscure. However, his conversion was simultaneously a call to preach Christ among the Gentiles (Gal 1:13–16), and for him this implied that righteousness did not come from observing the Jewish law. This suggests that he first persecuted the Christians

for preaching to the Gentiles and undermining the importance of the law, and then became one who did so himself.
If this is so, Paul's persecution indirectly reveals the existence of liberal Christians within a few years after the death
and resurrection of Jesus.

J. D. G. Dunn has argued that Mark 2:1–3:6 is a pre-
Markan and pre-Pauline unit of tradition which shows the
movement of some group within early Christianity toward
a liberal position, on the basis of stories about Jesus.

Whenever this liberal view first arose, it is clear that it
split the early church in two, since not all embraced it. And
this view created a decisive break between those Christians
who held it, and Judaism. Admission of Gentiles into the
church without requiring that they keep the Jewish law,
implied a new interpretation of the law and of Judaism itself according to which neither was as central to God's
dealings with the world as non-Christian Jews would
think. Or in other words, a liberal policy toward Gentile
converts to Christianity involved failure to adhere to the
Jewish law. When the most influential leaders of early
Christianity adopted the liberal position, the ultimate separation of Christianity from Judaism had begun.

Summary

The earliest church was composed of those followers
of Jesus who believed that he fulfilled Israel's expectation
of the messiah despite his crucifixion. This distinguished
the church from the rest of Israel, as did its peculiar interpretation of what it meant to be the messiah. However, the
eventual separation of the church from Israel resulted from
the very early adoption of the view by some Christians that

Gentiles could be members of the church without keeping the Jewish law. It was this group of Christians which non-Christian Jews first persecuted. The eventual predominance of this view among Christians was the chief factor in the separation of the church from Israel.

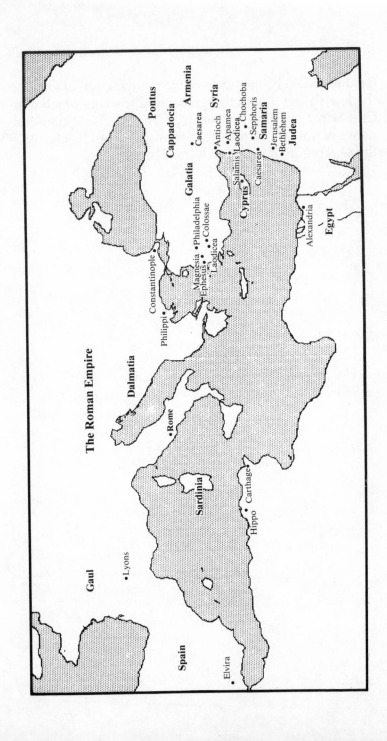

The Roman Empire

III.

CONSERVATIVE JEWISH CHRISTIANITY

That those who had a more conservative policy toward Gentile converts remained closely connected with Judaism until developments within Judaism separated them.

Introduction

In a certain sense the church was from the beginning conservative, but unconsciously so, taking the enduring validity of Judaism for granted. This implicit conservatism came to consciousness when the problem of how to treat Gentile converts first arose. At this point one part of the church abandoned its implicit conservative stance, and another part of the church embraced it explicitly. It seems clear that the conservative branch of the church remained more closely connected to Judaism than did the liberal branch. Of course, their belief that Jesus was the messiah distinguished the conservative Jewish Christians from the rest of Judaism, as we have already noted. But since conservative Jewish Christians adhered to the law, there was no essential barrier between them and non-Christian Jews. The two were not separate until developments within Judaism ended its tolerance of faith in Jesus.

We will trace the history of conservative Jewish Christianity from the time of the 'Apostolic Council' in 48 CE until the end of the fourth century. And we will distinguish two types of conservative Jewish Christians: on one hand, stable communities of conservative Jewish Christians; and on the other, members of the liberal branch of the church who wanted to keep some part of the Jewish law.

We hear of conservative Jewish Christians from Judea who were active at Antioch and participants in the 'Apostolic Council' in 48 CE. In the 50's and early 60's there were conservative Jewish Christian missionaries (perhaps from Judea) active in Galatia, Philippi, Colossae and perhaps Rome. The gospel of Matthew derives from a conservative Jewish Christian community in Antioch in the 80's. Likewise the gospel of John derives from such a community, perhaps at Ephesus in the 90's. A writer living in Rome in the second century, and a third century Syrian document, mention conservative Jewish Christians. We hear of a conservative Jewish Christian group called the Elkasaites in Rome and Caesarea in the third century. Another such group, the Ebionites, originated in Palestine and spread from there to Asia Minor, Rome and Cyprus. Writers living in Gaul in the second century, in North Africa, Rome and Caesarea in the third century, and in Palestine, Cyprus and North Africa in the fourth century, mention the Ebionites.

We hear of liberal Christians attracted to Jewish practices in Asia Minor and possibly Alexandria in the second century, in Caesarea in the third century, and in several places in the fourth century: Spain, Asia Minor and Syria.

All of these places, throughout this period, were part of the Roman empire. During this time there were at least two important developments. First, in Palestine the Jews revolted against Rome unsuccessfully in 66 CE and again in 132 CE. In quelling the first revolt, the Romans destroyed the temple; it was never rebuilt. As a result of the second, the Romans razed Jerusalem and forbade Jews to live there. In consequence of this threat to its survival, Judaism became intolerant of the conservative Jewish Christians and separated them from itself, a process reflected in the gospels of Matthew and John.

Second, Christianity, which was virtually unknown to the Roman empire at large in 48 CE, continued to grow and spread. Rome first persecuted the Christians and finally granted them toleration in the Edict of Milan during the reign of the emperor Constantine (305–337). In retrospect this was the beginning of a long-lasting alliance between church and state. At the time this was certainly less clear, as we can see from the unsuccessful attempt of the emperor Julian (361–363) to promote pagan religion and Judaism in opposition to Christianity. Temporarily at least, this seems to have had the effect of making Jewish practices attractive to Christians.

Though conservative Jewish Christianity was not as numerous or influential as liberal Christianity, it did derive from the earliest days of the church. In some places and at some times it must have been the only form of Christianity known. This is especially likely to have been the case in Syria.

Our information about the earlier part of this period comes from the works of Josephus, Tacitus and Suetonius which we have already mentioned. Another Roman historian of the period is Dio Cassius (c. 155–235) who wrote the history of Rome up to his own day.

Our chief source of information about the church in this period is the *Church History* of Eusebius (c. 260–339).

Our information about conservative Jewish Christians comes from the following sources:

1ST CENTURY—Letters of Paul
Paul opposes conservative Jewish Christians in:
Galatians (c. 53)
Romans (c. 56)
Philippians (c. 60)
Colossians (c. 60)

Acts of the Apostles (c. 85)

Letter of James
probably a product of conservative Jewish Christianity; exactly where and when is uncertain

Gospel of Matthew
product of a conservative Jewish Christian community, probably in Antioch in about 85

Gospel of John
product of a conservative Jewish Christian community, probably at Ephesus in about 95

2ND CENTURY—Letters of Ignatius of Antioch
after having been bishop of Antioch for some time, in about 107 he was taken to Rome to be executed; on his way he wrote to a number of churches of Asia Minor to thank them for their hospitality to him; he opposes conservative Jewish Christianity in *Magnesians; Philadelphians*

Letter of Barnabas
a document of uncertain date and author, perhaps composed in Alexandria; it opposes conservative Jewish Christianity

Justin Martyr (c. 100–165)
born in Samaria, he became a Christian while teaching at
Ephesus; eventually he opened a school of philosophy in
Rome and was martyred there; he mentions conservative
Jewish Christianity in *Dialogue with Trypho*

Celsus
mentions conservative Jewish Christians in his attack on
Christianity written in about 170: *True Doctrine*

Irenaeus (c. 130–200)
born in Asia Minor, he was a presbyter in Lyons in Gaul
and its bishop from 178 onward; he mentions conservative
Jewish Christians in *Against Heresies*

3RD CENTURY—Tertullian (160–230)
born in Carthage in North Africa, he became a Christian in
197; in 213 he became a Montanist, i.e., a member of a char-
ismatic Christian sect; he mentions conservative Jewish
Christianity in several writings

Hippolytus (170–236)
a presbyter at Rome; when Callistus II was elected pope in
217, Hippolytus was elected anti-pope; he was reconciled
to the church by Pope Pontian in 235 when both were exiled to Sardinia by the emperor Maximinus (235–238); he
refers to conservative Jewish Christianity in his *Refutation
of All Heresies*

Origen (185–254)
head of the catechetical school of Alexandria in Egypt from
about 203 to 231; in 231 he moved to Caesarea in Palestine

and founded another school there; he mentions conservative Jewish Christians in various writings

Didascalia
a document of uncertain date, probably composed in Syria, which discusses various persons and groups within the church, e.g., bishops, deacons, widows and orphans, and discusses various practices of the church, e.g., liturgy; its final chapter opposes conservative Jewish Christians

4TH CENTURY—Eusebius (c. 260–339)
bishop of Caesarea in Palestine from 314 onward; he mentions conservative Jewish Christians in *Church History; Onomastikon*

Council of Elvira (c. 305)
several of the canons of this synod, convened in Elvira in Spain, oppose conservative Jewish Christianity

Epiphanius (315–403)
born in Palestine, he was a monk in Palestine and Egypt and in 333 became head of a monastic community in Palestine; from 367 to 403 he was bishop of Salamis in Cyprus; he mentions conservative Jewish Christianity in *Against Heresies*

Clementine *Homilies* and *Recognitions*
two versions of the same basic story: Clement, a Roman citizen, goes to Palestine where he becomes a follower of the apostle Peter and journeys with him through Syria, and in the course of the journey is reunited with his mother, twin brothers and father, whom he had thought dead. Set within this framework, and comprising the greatest part of

each writing, are various discourses, many of them debates between Peter and Simon Magus who precedes Peter and his party through Syria. There is widespread agreement that the *Homilies* and *Recognitions* both depend on a basic document which is no longer extant, and it is further argued that this basic document made use of another document, the *Preaching of Peter*, as a source. Georg Strecker argues that the *Preaching of Peter* was written c. 200 CE. Thus the Clementine writings testify to the views of conservative Jewish Christians from 200 through the next several centuries during which the *Preaching of Peter* was used and reused, presumably by these Christians.

Basil (329–79)
born in Caesarea in Asia Minor, he founded a monastery in Pontus and lived there from 358 to 365; in 370 he became bishop of Caesarea; in two of his letters he mentions the conservative Jewish Christian views of Apollinaris, bishop of Laodicea in Syria

Apostolic Constitutions
a document of uncertain date, probably composed in Syria, which was compiled from the Didascalia and other similar church manuals; it ends with a series of canons, one of which opposes conservative Jewish Christianity

Council of Laodicea (between 343 and 381)
several of the canons of this synod, convened at Laodicea in Asia Minor, oppose conservative Jewish Christianity

Jerome (347–419)
born in Dalmatia, he traveled widely, finally settling in a monastery in Bethlehem in 386; there he devoted himself

to biblical scholarship; he mentions conservative Jewish Christians in several writings

John Chrysostom (349–407)
born in Antioch, he became a Christian in 369; from about 374 to 381 he was a hermit; he served as a presbyter in Antioch from 386 to 398; from 398 until he was exiled to Armenia in 404, he was patriarch of Constantinople; he opposed conservative Jewish Christianity in eight homilies delivered in Antioch in 386–387

Augustine (354–430)
born in North Africa, he spent some years in Italy and became a Christian there in 387; in 391 he became bishop of Hippo in North Africa; while a bishop, he lived in a monastic community; he mentions conservative Jewish Christians in *On Heresies*

Conservative Jewish Christianity
in the Letters of Paul and the Acts of the Apostles

The earliest explicit reference to conservative Jewish Christianity occurs in connection with the 'Apostolic Council' in Jerusalem. According to Acts 15:1–2 the occasion for the Council was that some Christians from Judea came to Antioch and taught that it was necessary to be circumcised in order to be saved. In order to settle the resulting debate, Paul and Barnabas went to Jerusalem to consult with the apostles and elders there. In his account of this meeting in Gal 2:1–10, Paul does not mention that conservative Jewish Christians who came to Antioch from Judea were the occasion for the meeting, but he does say that they were his opponents in the discussion, describing them as 'false brethren' who tried to 'bring us into bondage' (v 4; cf. Acts 15:5). Both accounts agree that the decision reached at the meeting was that Gentile Christians did not need to be circumcised. From that time on, the most important leaders of the church agreed on a liberal policy; however, there remained many Christians who continued to be conservative.

We next see them clearly as Paul's opponents in Galatia. Sometime after Paul founded the churches in Galatia, other missionaries came through Galatia, persuasively teaching the Galatians that in order to be Christians, they needed to be circumcised and keep the Jewish law (cf. Gal 4:21). However, these conservative Jewish Christian missionaries were not simply exponents of the law. They apparently did not hold that Christians had to keep the whole law (5:3) and they may have seen a connection between being under the law and the elemental spirits of the universe (4:3, 9). Here we see for the first time the syncretistic character of the conservative Jewish Christians, a feature of their thinking which we will see again.

Conservative Jewish Christians next appear as Paul's opponents in Philippi. In Phil 3:2–4:1 Paul warns the Philippians against those who urge circumcision and the keeping of the Jewish law on them. It is likely that these conservative Jewish Christians are missionaries like those Paul confronted in Galatia. In his letter to the Romans Paul makes an argument against conservative Jewish Christianity, but it is not clear that he is responding to a group of such Christians in Rome; he may simply be trying to explain his position on the question.

The letter to the Colossians (perhaps not written by Paul) also provides evidence of conservative Jewish Christianity. The letter opposes the Colossians' attraction to a 'philosophy' (2:8) which included, along with self-abase-

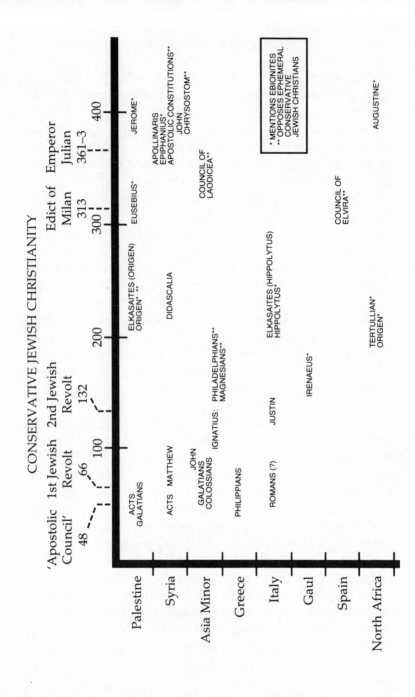

CONSERVATIVE JEWISH CHRISTIANITY

ment, worship of angels and visions (2:18), observation of (Jewish?) rules concerning food (2:16, 21), the celebration of festivals, new moons and sabbaths (2:16) and probably the practice of circumcision (cf. 2:11). Like the conservative Jewish Christians in Galatia, those in Colossae seem to have connected observance of the law with the elemental spirits of the universe (2:8). The syncretism of the latter is even more pronounced than that of the former.

Letter of James

Another probable example of conservative Jewish Christian thought is provided by the letter of James. In Acts and the letters of Paul the conservative Jewish Christians appear indirectly, as the opponents of the writers. However, the author of James himself seems to be a conservative Jewish Christian. The entire letter consists of ethical exhortation which is summed up as keeping the 'law of liberty' (1:25; 2:12). And this in turn is specified as loving your neighbor as yourself (2:8; cf. 4:11). In 2:8-12 the author argues that it is necessary to keep the whole law and uses as his example that one cannot avoid adultery but indulge in killing without becoming a transgressor of the law. Since the question of whether or not Gentile Christians are bound by the law does not arise explicitly, it is possible that James is simply addressed to Jewish Christians and does not espouse a conservative policy toward Gentiles. However, in view of the early origin of the Gentile question, it seems unlikely that the author could speak as he does even if he is writing for Jewish Christians, if he did not think what he said was also true for Gentiles. This is confirmed by his argument in 2:14-26 that faith must be complemented by works, an argument that seems directed

against Paul's position that Gentiles do not have to keep
the law.

Jewish Rejection of Jewish Christianity

Conservative Jewish Christianity was distinguished
from Judaism by its belief that Jesus was the messiah. This
distinction became a separation as a result of the failure of
the first Jewish revolution and the destruction of the temple in 70 CE. At this time in the history of Israel, there was
a good chance that the people of Israel might disappear
from the stage of history. That they did not was largely due
to the efforts of Rabbi Johanan ben Zakkai and his associates, who provided a new focal point for the people to replace the temple cult and the institutions connected with
it. On the negative side, there seems to have been an attempt to exclude deviant Jews, perhaps especially Jewish
Christians, in response to this crisis. Alan Segal has argued
that they were excluded in an important degree on Christological grounds, i.e., because they recognized Jesus as a
second power in heaven alongside God.

The attempt to exclude Jewish Christians (among others) seems to have taken the form of verbal assault, flog-
ging and exclusion from the synagogues. A principal
instrument for achieving the last of these was the addition
of a prayer to the synagogue liturgy, the *Birkat ha-Minim*
(Blessing of Heretics), in which heretics were cursed.
Rather than curse themselves, heretics would cease participation in the synagogue worship. According to the Babylonian Talmud, the authoritative collection of, and
commentary on, rabbinic law, this prayer was composed
by Rabbi Samuel the Small in response to a request from
Rabbi Gamaliel, the successor of Rabbi Johanan ben Zak-

kai, sometime between 85 and 95 CE (b. Ber 28b–29a). That Jewish Christians were included among the *minim* cursed in this prayer is suggested by a number of references to *minim* in rabbinic literature. For example, the Tosephta, another collection of rabbinic law, reports that Rabbi Eliezer ben Hyrcanus (c. 100) accounted for an accusation of heresy against him by recalling that he was once pleased when a certain Jacob repeated a saying of Jesus to him in the town of Sepphoris (T. Hull 2.24). The Babylonian Talmud (b. A.Z. 16b–17a) and Qoheleth Rabbah, a rabbinic commentary on Ecclesiastes (Qoheleth Rabbah 1.8.4), also contain this story, with some variations.

The gospels of Matthew and John seem to have been produced among groups of conservative Jewish Christians who were receiving treatment such as this at the hands of non-Christian Jews.

Gospel of Matthew

The chief representative of a conservative Jewish Christian position in the New Testament is the gospel of Matthew. Matthew's failure to explain Jewish customs and terms (cf. Matt 15:1–20 compared with Mark 7:1–23; Matt 23:5; 5:22) and his use of 'kingdom of heaven' instead of 'kingdom of God,' apparently to avoid mentioning God, as was the pious practice among Jews, suggest that Matthew derives from a Jewish milieu. That Matthew is a conservative Jewish Christian gospel seems likely because it presents Jesus as affirming the continuing validity of the law (5:17–20). Jesus does go on to reinterpret the law (5:21–48) but his reinterpretations make the law more demanding, so the old commands are included in the new. Jesus also affirms the oral law, taught by the scribes and Pharisees

(23:2), but again reinterprets it (23:16–22; cf. 12:1–4; 15:1–20; 19:3–9). That the law as reinterpreted by Jesus is binding on Gentile Christians is clear from the great commission with which the gospel ends. In it Jesus commands his disciples to make disciples of all nations, teaching them to observe all he has commanded them (28:19–20).

However, even as Matthew provides the strongest affirmation of the continuing validity of the Jewish law for Gentile Christians to be found in the New Testament, it also reflects a high degree of hostility between Jews and Christians. The most striking example of this is Jesus' woes against the Pharisees in Matt 23. This probably reflects tension between Christians and Pharisees in Matthew's own day, as well as Jesus' conflict with them. Along with such expressions of Christian hostility to the Jews, Matthew also indicates that Christians were being persecuted by the Jews (cf. Matt 23:29–39; 10:16–33; 5:10–12).

Gospel of John

Although the gospel of John does not clearly embrace a conservative Jewish Christian position, as Matthew does, it seems likely that the former is also a product of conservative Jewish Christianity. References to the possibility that believers in Jesus be excluded from the synagogue (9:22; 12:42; 16:2) suggest that until recently the Johannine Christians have been part of a synagogue which also included non-Christian Jews. A short time before the writing of the gospel, however, the Christian Jews have begun to be expelled from the synagogue, probably as part of the Jewish retrenchment after the destruction of the temple in 70 CE which is also reflected in Matthew. In both cases this has produced considerable hostility on the part of the Christian

Jews toward the non-Christian Jews. The most striking evidence of this in John is the frequent characterization of the opponents of Jesus in the gospel as 'the Jews.' This would certainly be an inadequate designation of the historical opponents of Jesus since it would not distinguish them from Jesus himself or from his adherents. But it is hardly less surprising as a reflection of the way the Johannine community designated its opponents; before their expulsion from the synagogue, they must have identified themselves as Jews. This usage seems to reflect the extreme hostility caused by the expulsion of the Christian Jews and the consequent rejection of any continuing identification of themselves as Jews by the Johannine community. However, there is some suggestion that the Johannine community did identify itself as Israel (1:31, 47, 49; 3:10; 12:13).

The chief indication that John is a product of conservative Jewish Christianity is that it is greatly concerned with the law, yet almost completely silent about the behavioral prescriptions of the law. For John the law comes into question almost entirely from a Christological perspective. Thus the law is seen mainly as a witness to Jesus, predicting his coming and even the details of his career (1:45; 2:22; 5:45–47; 7:42, 52; 12:34; 13:18; 15:25; 17:12; 20:9). And when the question of Jesus' conformity to the prescriptions of the law arises, it is always subordinated to the acceptance of Jesus as fulfillment of the law (cf. 5:9–18; 7:19–24; 9:13–17; 10:33–36; 19:7). Faith in Jesus rests on a correct interpretation of the law, and the exact nature of such a correct interpretation is at the center of John's debate with 'the Jews.' In this context John's virtual silence about the behavioral prescriptions of the law suggests strongly that the Johannine Christians were in agreement on this point with the non-Christian Jews with whom they were struggling, i.e., that they observed the law in the same way as the non-

Christian Jews. If in addition to their extravagant claims about Jesus, the Johannine Christians abandoned observance of the law, it seems that this would have emerged more clearly as a point of dispute. This would be especially true if, as Raymond Brown has argued, the gospel is partly an attempt to convince crypto-Christians who are still within the synagogue to declare their faith in Jesus and be expelled from the synagogue. If this involved not only belief in Jesus, but also abandonment of observing the law, we would surely expect explicit argument for the latter.

Raymond Brown also argues that the Johannine community includes Gentiles. The clearest indication of this is that terms such as rabbi and messiah are explained (1:38; 20:16; 1:41; 4:25). If this is correct, then it would seem that the Gentiles are probably also observing the Jewish law. If they were not, we would expect their admission to the community without keeping the law to be a point of contention between the Johannine community and the non-Christian Jews.

This indirect argument that the Johannine community consisted of conservative Jewish Christians receives some support from the treatment of Jesus' disputes about the law in John. It is true that Jesus several times refers to the law as belonging to 'the Jews' (8:17; 10:34; 15:25). But this does not seem to indicate complete abandonment of the law by the Johannine community. When the question of Jesus' observance of the law arises, it is subordinated to Christological interests, as we have already noted. This is clearest in 5:1–18 where Jesus defends himself for healing on the sabbath by arguing that God works on the sabbath, and that Jesus does what the Father does. But even here the sabbath law seems to be taken seriously; the argument is not that the sabbath law is obsolete, but rather that it does not apply to Jesus in the way one might first think it did. This implicit recognition of the validity of the law is even more apparent in 7:21–24 where Jesus defends his healing on the sabbath by comparing it to circumcision which is permitted on the sabbath. In 10:31–39 Jesus defends his (implicit) claim to be God by referring to Ps 82:6 where others are referred to as gods. Passages like these support the view that the Johannine community, including its Gentile members, continues to observe the law. However, it is clear that even if this is so, the law does not have the central place for the Johannine community which it has for the Matthean community. For the former the law (and virtually everything else) is completely eclipsed by Jesus (cf. 1:17). It may be that the references to the law as belonging to 'the Jews,' which we have noted above, indicate a movement away from observance of the law by the Johannine community, a movement occasioned by its alienation from non-Christian Jews.

Conservative Jewish Christianity
in Justin's *Dialogue with Trypho*, Celsus' *True Doctrine* and the Didascalia

The epistle of James, and even more clearly the gospels of Matthew and John, seem to derive from communities of conservative Jewish Christians. We hear direct references to such communities in the writings of Justin Martyr (c. 100–165) and Celsus. In his *Dialogue with Trypho*, written in Rome in about 160 but presenting an account of a discussion in Ephesus with a Jew named Trypho, Justin refers to Jewish Christians who compel Gentile Christians to live in all respects according to the law given by Moses. Justin does not approve of such Christians and seems to imply that they will not be saved (*Dial.* 47). In his *True Doctrine*, written about 170 CE, Celsus, a pagan critic of Christianity, mentions the existence of Christians who desire to live as Jews according to the Mosaic law (in Origen, *Against Celsus* 5.61). However, they must not be typical of the Christians known to Celsus because one of his criticisms of Christianity is that it has abandoned the Jewish law (ibid. 2.1–4). The third century Didascalia also makes reference to conservative Jewish Christians whom it opposes.

Elkasaites, Ebionites, Cerinthians

Some groups of conservative Jewish Christians are known to us by name. One of these is the Elkasaites, who are mentioned in the writings of Hippolytus (170–236), Origen (185–254) and Epiphanius (315–403). Elkasai appeared in the third year of the emperor Trajan, i.e., 101 CE (Hippolytus, *Refutations* 9.13.3–4) and produced a book, fragments of which are preserved by Hippolytus and Epiphanius. According to Hippolytus the Elkasaites believed that Christians are obliged to be circumcised and to live according to the law (ibid. 9.14). Origen says that they rejected the apostle Paul (in Eusebius, *Church History* 6.38). According to Epiphanius the book of Elkasai rejected sacrifice and priestly rites and claimed that they had never been offered to God at all according to the fathers and the law (*Against Heresies* 19.3.6). This selective adherence to the law, which was also characteristic of the conservative Jewish Christians in Galatia, may be an adjustment to the destruction of the temple in Jerusalem in 70 CE, which made the sacrificial cult impossible. The book of Elkasai was brought to Rome by a certain Alcibiades of Apamea in 220 (Hippolytus, *Refutations* 9.13.1), and Origen reports that the movement was promoted in Caesarea in 247 (in Eusebius, *Church History* 6.38). The book remained current, presumably among conservative Jewish Christians, for several centuries, as the references to it by later writers indicate.

The best known group of conservative Jewish Christians is the Ebionites. They were first mentioned by Irenaeus (c. 130–200), bishop of Lyons, in *Against Heresies*. Irenaeus says that they use only the gospel according to Matthew and reject Paul as an apostate from the law. They practice circumcision and observe the law (1.26.2). It is not completely clear from this that they had a conservative policy toward Gentile converts, but this is strongly suggested by their opposition to Paul, since he argued that Gentiles should be free from the law. Tertullian (160–230) several times refers to a certain Ebion as the founder of the group (*On Prescription of Heretics* 33; *On the Flesh of Christ* 14, 18, 24; *On Veiling Virgins* 6). Hippolytus says that the Ebionites thought they were justified by keeping the law (*Refutations* 7.34; 10.22); he also refers to Ebion (ibid. 7.35). A work *Against All Heresies*, falsely attributed to Tertullian, explains Ebion's observance of the law as based on Matt 10:24—'No disciple is above his master, nor a servant above his lord' (3). Origen correctly understands that the name 'Ebionites' does not derive from a founder named Ebion, but from a Hebrew word meaning 'poor' (cf. *On First Principles* 4.3.8; *Against Celsus* 2.1). Origen mentions the Ebionites' practice of circumcision (*Homily on Genesis* 3.5), their observance of the laws concerning pure and impure food (*On Matthew* 11.12), their celebration of passover in imitation of Jesus (*Commentary on Matthew* 79), and their rejection of Paul (*Against Celsus* 5.65; *Homily on Jeremiah* 17.2) which continues to his own day (*Homily on Jeremiah* 19). Origen says that they appealed to Matt 15:24—'I was sent to the lost sheep of the house of Israel' (*On First Prin-*

ciples 4.3.8). According to Origen some Ebionites thought that Jesus was the son of Joseph and Mary; others accepted the virgin birth (*Against Celsus* 5.61; cf. *On Matthew* 16.12).

Eusebius (c. 260–339) repeats many of the observations of Origen, adding that the Ebionites observe the sabbath and celebrate the resurrection of the Lord on Sunday (*Church History* 3.27; cf. 6.17). Eusebius also says that the Ebionites lived in a village called Choba (probably = Chochoba, a village in Palestine) (*Onomastikon*). Epiphanius devotes a chapter of his *Against Heresies* to the Ebionites. He repeats Eusebius' statement that the Ebionites lived in Chochoba (30.2.8) and adds that the group spread from there to Asia Minor, Rome and Cyprus (30.18.1). Epiphanius also adds to the reports of earlier writers about the Ebionites the information that they avoided touching anyone of another nation, washed after sexual intercourse and required marriage (30.2.3–6), that they washed daily and abstained from meat (30.15.3), that they rejected sacrifice (30.16.5–7) and that they rejected the prophets of the Hebrew scripture (30.15.2; 30.18.4, 9) and parts of the pentateuch (30.18.7–9). Epiphanius also says that they rejected Paul, arguing that he was a Gentile who became a Jew in order to marry a Jewish woman; when he could not marry her, he argued against Judaism (30.16.8–9). Jerome (347–419) refers frequently to the Ebionites without adding anything to what we have already noted (cf. *On Galatians* 5:3; *On Matthew* 12:2). Augustine (354–430) also mentions them (*On Heresies* 10), as do several other writers.

According to Epiphanius the Ebionites made use of a special gospel; Epiphanius quotes a number of passages (*Against Heresies* 30.13, 14, 16, 22). This gospel resembles the synoptic gospels and was probably written in the first half of the second century. According to Eusebius (*Church History* 6.17) Symmachus, an Ebionite, made a Greek translation of the Hebrew scriptures during the reign of the emperor Septimius Severus (193–211). As we shall see, it is likely that the Clementine *Homilies* and *Recognitions* are Ebionite in origin.

Epiphanius also describes the Cerinthians as conservative Jewish Christians. He reports that they believed that just as Jesus was circumcised and lived according to the law, so his disciples should do the same (*Against Heresies* 28.5.1–3). This same understanding of the Cerinthians is also found in many later writers. But Irenaeus (*Against Heresies* 1.26.1), Hippolytus (*Refutations* 7.33) and Eusebius (*Church History* 3.28) give earlier descriptions of the Cerinthians, and they do not say that the Cerinthians were conservative Jewish Christians. It seems likely that Epiphanius and those who followed him were mistaken about the conservative Jewish Christian character of the Cerinthians.

Clementine *Homilies* and *Recognitions*

The only direct information about conservative Jewish Christians in post-New Testament times is provided by the fourth century Clementine *Homilies* and *Recognitions*. These two writings seem to derive from a basic document which, in turn, made use of another document, the *Preaching of Peter* (c. 200). Epiphanius claims to have had access to an Ebionite writing called the *Journeys of Peter* (*Against Heresies* 30.15.1). This may be the basic document underlying the *Homilies* and *Recognitions*. If so, then the *Preaching of Peter* and its subsequent recensions testify to the views of the Ebionites.

In *Homilies* 8.6–7 the teaching of Moses is identified with the teaching of Jesus, which means that God accepts those who believe in either. This implies that following the Christian life is the same as keeping the law of Moses. This is explicit in *Homilies* 4.7 and 22, where Clement's conversion to Christianity is described as living after the manner of the Jews or accepting the law of the Jews. Many specific regulations of Jewish law are mentioned as being incumbent on Christians in *Homilies* 7.4 and 8; 11.28, 30 and 33; and the letter of Peter to James 4.1. These include abstinence from the table of devils, from dead flesh, from blood, from animals that have been suffocated or caught by wild beasts, washing from all pollutions, including sexual intercourse and menstruation, and the practice of circumcision.

However, despite their conservative character, the Clementine *Homilies* and *Recognitions* do not accept the Jewish law entirely. The *Homilies* argue that the law contains false passages, introduced into the law after Moses gave it orally, when it was written down. This was done by the evil one, but for a good purpose, namely to divide the wicked, who would believe the false passages, from the good who would not (*Homilies* 2.38). The false passages are chiefly those which speak negatively of God. They include passages which suggest that there is more than one God, or that God is ignorant and does not have foreknowledge, or that God is fond of sacrifice, as well as others (*Homilies* 2.42–4). These false passages can be identified both by their incongruity with the teaching of Jesus and by rational argumentation based on creation (*Homilies* 3.48). The *Recognitions* knows nothing of this theory of false passages in the law, but has a somewhat comparable idea, namely that the true prophet (Jesus) would abolish the temple and the sacrificial cult. These were instituted by Moses as a first step toward weaning the people from the worship of false gods, but were eventually to be abolished by the true prophet (*Recognitions* 1.36–7). Georg Strecker and others have suggested that the part of the *Recognitions* which presents this theory (i.e., 1.33–71) derives from another Ebionite source which Epiphanius mentions, namely the *Ascents of James* (*Against Heresies* 30.16.6–9). Hans-Joachim Schoeps has argued that the theory that there are false passages in the law is an Ebionite response to the views of Marcion and the Gnostics (see pp. 96–101 below).

Ephemeral Conservative Jewish Christianity

We have thus far been considering the history of well-defined communities of conservative Jewish Christians (and their apostles). In addition to these groups, we can also see that again and again Gentile Christians were attracted to Judaism and began to adopt Jewish practices. We can see an early example of this in the favorable reception accorded conservative missionaries in the Pauline churches. Later examples of this ephemeral conservative Jewish Christianity often arose through contact between a Christian community and the local Jewish community, or even as a result of proselytism by the latter.

This type of conservative Jewish Christianity seems to be reflected in the letters of Ignatius of Antioch (c. 107) and the Letter of Barnabas (c. 70–140). In his letters to the churches at Magnesia and Philadelphia, Ignatius seems concerned to oppose ephemeral conservative Jewish Christianity. In Philad 6.1 he says, 'If anyone interpret Judaism to you, do not listen to him.' This seems to reflect some tendency on the part of the Philadelphians to adopt Jewish practices. Since Ignatius goes on to refer to hearing Judaism from the uncircumcised, it seems that the Philadelphians who are attracted to Judaism have not gone so far as to be circumcised (cf. Rev 3:9). And in Magn 8.1 he says that living according to Judaism at the present time would be a confession that we have not received grace, and in 10.3 that it is monstrous to talk of Jesus Christ and practice Judaism. Very probably he is here too speaking about Gentile Christians who want to keep the Jewish law. Similarly, the entire message of the Letter of Barnabas, as we shall see in some detail below, is a warning against being shipwrecked by conversion to their law (3.6).

Origen argues in his homilies against the observance of Jewish practices such as circumcision, fasting and the keeping of the sabbath and festivals by his congregation (cf. *Homilies on Joshua* 20.6; *on Matthew* 12.5; *on Jeremiah* 12.12 (13); *on Leviticus* 7.5; 10.2). Apparently they had some significant inclination to the contrary. Origen attributes this inclination to the activity of Jewish missionaries (*Commentary on Matthew* ser. 16). The fourth century Council of Elvira, Spain condemned Christian observance of Jewish practices (Canons 26, 49, 50) as did the *Apostolic Constitutions* which says, 'If a bishop or another cleric fasts with the Jews or feasts with them or receives gifts from their festivals, as unleavened bread or something else, let him be purified; if it is a layperson, let him be excommunicated' (8.47.70; 65). Similarly, the fourth century canons of Laodicea oppose Christian observance of Jewish practices; the 29th of them says that Christians found Judaizing will be shut out from Christ (see also canon 16). According to Basil of Caesarea in Asia Minor (329–79), Apollinaris (310–90), the bishop of Laodicea, who is more famous for his Christological views, also looked for the renewal of the Jerusalem temple and the observance of worship according to the law (Letter 265.2), the return of circumcision, observance of the sabbath and a general return to Judaism (263.4).

And Christians who partly observed the Jewish law provided the occasion for John Chrysostom (349–407) to deliver eight homilies against them in 386–87 in Antioch. In these homilies he attacks those Christians who were drawn to participation in synagogue worship, especially its festivals and fasts, and even to circumcision.

The apparent resurgence of ephemeral conservative Jewish Christianity in the fourth century may have been stimulated by the emperor Julian (361–63) who intended to rebuild the temple in Jerusalem and return the city to the Jews. However, even without such a stimulus, Christians have been attracted to Jewish practices again and again in the history of the church, even up to the present. A well-known contemporary example is provided by the Seventh Day Adventists who keep holy the sabbath, rather than Sunday.

Summary

After the question of how to treat Gentile converts to Christianity arose in the early years of the church's existence, one branch of the church became explicitly conservative, i.e., it required that Gentile converts keep the Jewish law. Perhaps because this was not the most influential position, it is largely visible somewhat indirectly in the New Testament as the position rejected in Acts and by Paul. However, the letter of James and the gospels of Matthew and John seem to be direct representatives of this position. The latter are especially illuminating because they show the growing separation of conservative Jewish Christianity from Judaism; in the aftermath of the destruction of the temple in 70 CE, Judaism was distancing itself from fringe movements such as Jewish Christianity.

In the second through the fourth centuries, conservative Jewish Christianity is again visible indirectly for the most part in the arguments of its opponents against it. The chief exception to this is the Clementine *Homilies* and *Recognitions*, which were written by conservative Jewish Christians. In addition to stable groups of conservative Jewish Christians, we also know that during this time Judaism exercised a strong attraction on many Christians, making them ephemeral conservative Christians.

Whenever we have more than minimal information about the views of these conservative Jewish Christians, we discover that they combined their affirmation of the continuing validity of the law with a special interpretation of it or criticism of a part of it. They also seem to have been especially open to syncretism.

Though conservative Jewish Christianity was rejected by the most influential circles of early Christianity, and also by Judaism, it continued to flourish for centuries, much longer than we are usually aware. This may be partly a result of the intrinsic rationality of combining belief in Jesus with observance of the Jewish law.

IV.

LIBERAL JEWISH CHRISTIANITY

That the liberal branch of the church was first composed of Jewish Christians who retained a positive view of Judaism despite holding that Gentile Christians were not bound by the law.

Introduction

The early church split into conservative and liberal branches over the question of whether or not Gentile converts to Christianity were bound by the Jewish law. It is probable that at the time of the 'Apostolic Council' (c. 48 CE) both branches of the church consisted mainly of Jewish Christians. However, probably because of its policy toward Gentile converts, the liberal branch of the church rapidly absorbed Gentiles and rather soon became a Gentile church. We will consider the consequences of this development below.

It is only during the first century CE that liberal Jewish Christians were a dominant force in the liberal branch of the church. Liberal Jewish Christians are mentioned as minority groups in the second century and make a final appearance in the fourth century.

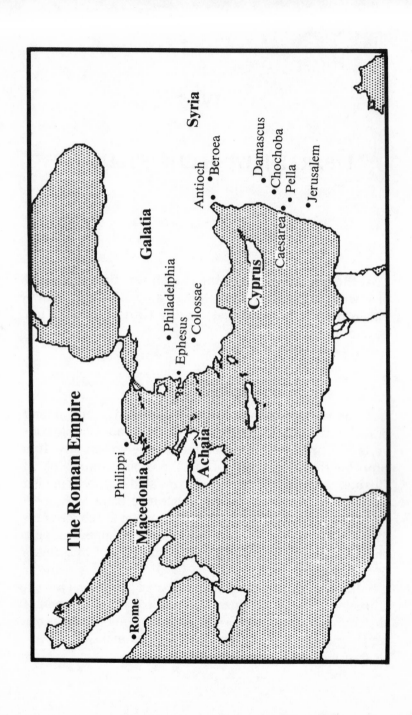

From the Acts of the Apostles and the letters of Paul we know of many liberal Jewish Christians in the early days of the church. We have already referred to Luke's presentation of Peter as the first to admit a Gentile to the church without requiring circumcision—the centurion Cornelius at Caesarea. It seems fairly certain that the Christians persecuted by Paul (in Jerusalem and Damascus, according to Acts) were liberal Jewish Christians. We can be sure that at least from the time of the 'Apostolic Council' the leaders of the church in Jerusalem, i.e., Peter, James and John, were liberal Jewish Christians. And we know the names of many other members of this branch of the church, especially the associates of Paul (e.g., Barnabas and Timothy).

The most important representative of liberal Jewish Christianity known to us is the apostle Paul. According to Acts he was a leader in the church at Antioch (13:1) and along with Barnabas evangelized the cities of Cyprus and central Asia Minor (13–14). Both Acts and Paul's letters witness to his evangelization of the cities of Macedonia and Achaia, and of western Asia Minor. According to Acts, Paul continued to evangelize even as a prisoner in Rome (28:17–31). Thus during the 40's, 50's and 60's of the first century the Pauline mission was responsible for the spread of Christianity throughout much of the Roman empire. From a somewhat later time in the first century Luke-Acts and the letter to the Hebrews also derive from liberal Jewish Christianity. Both are somehow connected with Paul.

In the second century we hear of liberal Jewish Christianity in Asia Minor and from Justin Martyr who wrote in Rome. In the fourth century we hear of a liberal Jewish Christian group called the Nazoraeans who lived in Syria in the city of Beroea (present-day Aleppo).

As we will see, the rapid decline of liberal Jewish

Christianity was partly the result of the unsuccessful Jewish rebellions against Rome in 66 and 132 CE. And the growth of Christianity among Gentiles, which eventually resulted in its acceptance by the Roman empire, was also a factor in this decline.

Our information about the Roman empire during this period comes from the historians Josephus, Tacitus, Suetonius and Dio Cassius. We learn about the church during this time chiefly from Eusebius and from Hegesippus (died c. 180), an earlier church historian quoted by Eusebius.

Our information about liberal Jewish Christians comes from the following sources:

1ST CENTURY—Letters of Paul
Paul presents the liberal Jewish Christian position in:
Galatians (c. 53)
Romans (c. 56)
Philippians (c. 60)
Colossians (c. 60)
Ephesians (?)

Luke–Acts (c. 85)
product of liberal Jewish Christianity; place of composition is uncertain

Letter to Hebrews
probably a product of liberal Jewish Christianity; author, place and exact time of composition are unknown

2ND CENTURY—Letters of Ignatius of Antioch
Ignatius may mention liberal Jewish Christians in *Philadelphians*

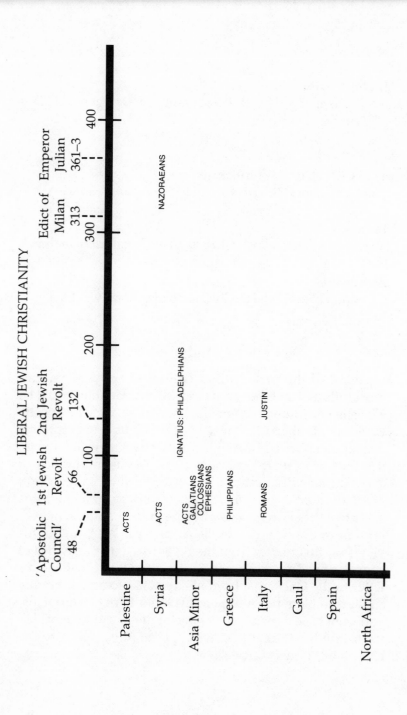

LIBERAL JEWISH CHRISTIANITY

Justin Martyr
mentions liberal Jewish Christianity in *Dialogue with Trypho; Apology*

4TH CENTURY—Epiphanius
mentions liberal Jewish Christians in *Against Heresies*

Jerome
mentions liberal Jewish Christians in *Commentary on Isaiah*

Augustine
mentions liberal Jewish Christians in several writings

Paul

One of the earliest, and easily the best known and most influential of those who argued that Gentiles could be Christians without keeping the Jewish law, was the apostle Paul. He had been an exceedingly zealous Jew before his conversion (Gal 1:14). As I have already suggested above, it seems likely that Paul persecuted the liberal branch of early Christianity because he perceived it as an attack on Judaism; then as a result of his conversion he joined this branch of the church, becoming the great champion of freedom from the law for Gentile Christians. We know of his views on this matter from his response to the activities of conservative Jewish Christian missionaries in Galatia in his letter to the Galatians, from his response to an apparently similar problem in Philippi in his letter to the Philippians, and from his extensive discussion of the question in his letter to the Romans, the exact application of which to the church in Rome is unclear.

Paul's arguments against the conservative position in Galatians include an appeal to the Galatians' experience of receiving the spirit when they believed in his message and thus without keeping the law (Gal 3:1–5). More importantly he proposes an interpretation of God's dealing with Israel according to which faith takes precedence over works of the law. According to Paul it is God's promise to Abraham which forms the basic structure of his saving plan, a promise which is based on faith, and which the law, coming 430 years later, does not alter or replace (3:6–18). This argument is based on perceiving a contradiction between the scriptural affirmation that life comes through faith (e.g., Hab 2:4) and the affirmation that life comes through keeping the law (e.g., Lev 18:5) (cf. Gal 3:11–12). Paul resolves the contradiction by arguing that the former (i.e., the covenant with Abraham) is primary and the latter (i.e., the Sinai covenant) secondary. Paul makes the same point in Gal 4:21–31 by means of an allegorical interpretation of Abraham's two sons and their mothers. Isaac and Sarah represent the covenant with Abraham; Ishmael and Hagar represent the Sinai covenant.

In Romans Paul repeats this argument based on the promise made to Abraham (Rom 4), but places it within a larger framework. In Rom 1–3 Paul argues that all, both Jew and Gentile, have sinned and are in need of salvation through Christ (cf. 3:21–26); thus keeping the law has not led to salvation for Israel and need not be undertaken by the Gentiles. Both receive salvation through fulfillment of the promises to Abraham.

In Philippians Paul argues that Christians must put confidence in Christ and not in the flesh, i.e., observance of the law, and he uses his own conversion as an example of doing so (Phil 3:2–11). This is probably one of Paul's underlying intentions in Gal 1–2 where he also tells the story of his conversion. The argument in Philippians brings to light most clearly why Paul is so opposed to Gentiles' keeping the Jewish law: as he sees it, keeping the law is a failure to trust that God can save Gentiles freely, without their achieving righteousness themselves by keeping the law.

The letter to the Colossians presents a similar argument against Gentile Christians' keeping of the law. Here the author (who may not be Paul) argues that such things as the sabbath are a shadow of what is to come, while the substance is Christ (2:16–17). In Christ the Colossians already have everything; keeping the law can add nothing (2:9–10). To do so is implicitly to deny the fullness of God in Christ.

Since Paul argues that keeping the law is not necessary for participation in God's salvation of the human race, he is left with the problem of why it was ever given. And Paul does not shrink from a radical answer to this question. In Gal 3:19–4:11 Paul says that the law was given for the sake of transgressions, to consign all things to sin, to be our custodian until the coming of Christ. In Rom 5:20–21 Paul makes clear what this means; he says that law came in to increase sin. In Rom 7 Paul explains how the law increased sin: the commandments awakened in us a desire for the opposite of what was commanded; in this way they became a means by which sin enslaved us. Thus Paul sees the law as having a negative role in God's plan for the human race; the law was intended to increase sin in order to make people ready to accept salvation in Christ. This is a radical reversal of the Jewish view of the law, a view which Paul undoubtedly shared before becoming a Christian. But for Paul God's salvation of the Gentiles without their keeping the law requires this new understanding of the law.

It is easy to forget that Paul addresses these arguments to Gentile Christians. He makes it quite clear that Gentiles are not to keep the law, but he nowhere says what he expects Jewish Christians to do. It is clear that for Paul they cannot regard the law as salvific, but it is not clear that they may not keep the law simply as a matter of continuing to be Jews. Abandonment of the Jewish law by Jewish Christians might seem to follow from Paul's understanding of the place of the law in the scheme of salvation, or to be implied by his own abandonment of the law (cf. Gal 4:12). But on the other hand Jewish Christians who would keep the law with its negative purpose would also have the antidote in their faith in Christ. And Paul's abandonment of the law may be a result of his subordination of all to the demands of apostleship, a subordination which can also lead him to keep the law (cf. 1 Cor 9:19–23; 2 Cor 11:24). If we take the latter as our starting point, Paul's own example may not be indicative of what he would have asked of other Jewish Christians (cf. 1 Cor 7:17–18; Gal 5:3).

Though it remains unclear whether or not Paul would have said that Jewish Christians might keep the law, it is clear that he retained a sense of the priority of Israel. As we have seen, he argues that Jew and Gentile equally need salvation through Christ, and he says that in Christ there is no Jew or Gentile (Gal 3:28; 1 Cor 12:13; Col 3:11). Still he can say that the order is 'Jew first and also the Greek' (Rom 2:9–10) and that the advantage of the Jew and the value of circumcision is 'much in every way' (Rom 3:1–2). And he presents Israel as the olive tree onto which the Gentiles are grafted, and warns the Gentiles not to boast over the branches which have been removed to make a place for them, i.e., unbelieving Jews (Rom 11:17–24). Similarly the author of Ephesians (who may not be Paul) reminds Gentile Christians that once they were far from the commonwealth of Israel and without God in the world, and that they have been brought near by Christ (Eph 2:11–22). Such passages seem to reflect a tendency on the part of the Gentiles who have become members of the church without keeping the law to forget the place of Israel in God's plan of salvation. Finally, Paul also says that in the end all Israel will be saved (Rom 11:25–26). This concern for the priority of Israel may make it likely that Paul would have seen a value in observance of the law by Jewish Christians as a way of maintaining their identity as Israel.

Luke-Acts

Luke-Acts provides the other important example of a liberal Jewish Christian viewpoint in the New Testament. Though it has long been almost taken for granted that Luke is a Gentile, today there is a growing tendency to see him as a Jew. The main reason for this is his understanding of the relationship between Jews and Gentiles in the church. It is first of all clear that for Luke the Gentile Christians need not keep the Jewish law. This follows most of all from Luke's account of the Apostolic Council in Acts 15, to which we have referred previously. It is interesting to see, however, that Luke does not argue this position, as Paul does, by showing that the law is not primary in the scheme of salvation. Rather Luke sees inclusion of Gentiles in the church without requiring them to keep the law as part of the fulfillment of God's promises to Israel. According to those promises, when God brought salvation to Israel, it would also become available to the Gentiles. They would be a people associated with the redeemed and restored Israel (Acts 15:13–18). This conception underlies Luke's version of the final decision of the Apostolic Council. In his account of this meeting in Galatians 2, Paul implies that it was agreed that the Gentiles would be completely free from the law. By contrast, according to Luke the Gentiles were to avoid idols, unchastity, what is strangled and blood (Acts 15:20, 29). In saying this Luke seems to be referring to the commandments in Leviticus 17–18 which are enjoined not only on Israel but also on the Gentiles living in their midst. Thus Gentile Christians, as a people associated with the redeemed Israel, keep those laws which apply to Gentiles in the midst of Israel. However, from the rest of the law they are free.

In Luke-Acts it is clear, as it is not in Paul, that Jewish Christians continue to keep the law. This is stated most clearly in Acts 21:20 where James and the elders of the church in Jerusalem point out to Paul the tens of thousands of Jewish Christians in Jerusalem, all zealous for the law. These Jewish Christians are concerned that Paul may be telling the Jews among the Gentiles to forsake the law (v 21). In order to show these Jewish Christians that they are mistaken about him, Paul undertakes a notable act of Jewish piety (v 22–26). Here and elsewhere Luke is concerned to show that Paul himself is entirely faithful to the law (cf. Acts 16:1–3; 25:8; 28:17). It seems likely that his portrayal of Paul is designed to persuade liberal Jewish Christians that Paul is himself a faithful Jew and does nothing to undermine the fidelity to the law of other Jews.

Hebrews

A final example of liberal Jewish Christianity in the New Testament may be seen in the 'letter' to the Hebrews. Though the 'letter' clearly presents an argument against the law, it is not clear that it is an argument that Gentiles should not keep it, or that anyone should not keep it (but cf. 13:9–11). The argument deals explicitly only with the temple cult which may have become a purely historical matter already by the time Hebrews was written, or, at any rate, soon would. It is also not clear that it is Jewish in origin, though this is strongly suggested by the detailed discussion of the temple cult (cf. also 1:1).

The argument against the law in Hebrews is basically that the law is part of a covenant which has been replaced by a new covenant. The author's main argument for this point of view is found in chapters 7:1–10:18. The starting point for the argument is that Jesus is high priest according to the order of Melchizedek (5:6, quoting Ps 110:4). For the author this implies that perfection was not obtainable through the Levitical priesthood upon which the law was established (7:11), and a change in priesthood means a change in law (7:12). Thus in the appointment of Jesus as high priest the law is set aside because of its weakness and uselessness, and a better hope is introduced (7:18–19).

The author explains the inferiority of the Levitical priesthood as a matter of its ministering in a copy of the true sanctuary in which Christ ministers (8:5–7; 10:1), and argues its inferiority by quoting Jer 31:31–34—the promise of a new convenant—arguing that a new covenant would not be necessary if the old one were not deficient (8:8–13). Viewing the Levitical priesthood as ministering in a copy of the true sanctuary clearly establishes its inferiority to the ministry of Christ in the true sanctuary, but also grants it a positive value as an anticipation of the good things to come (10:1).

Liberal Jewish Christianity
in the Letters of Ignatius of Antioch
and Justin's *Dialogue with Trypho*

Ignatius of Antioch may refer to liberal Jewish Christians when he speaks of hearing Christianity from the circumcised (Philad 6.1). In context it seems fairly clear that these are Jewish Christians who do not require that Gentile Christians be circumcised, but we cannot be sure that they continued to practice Judaism themselves. Justin Martyr clearly refers to liberal Jewish Christians. He mentions the existence of Jewish Christians who keep the law themselves but do not require Gentile Christians to keep it (*Dial.* 47).

The Nazoraeans

The last clear appearance of a community of liberal Jewish Christians on the stage of history is probably to be seen in the Nazoraeans. Epiphanius is the first to mention this group of Jewish Christians, who apparently lived in Beroea in Syria during his day (*Against Heresies* 29.7.7). According to him they observed the law and circumcision (29.5.4; 7.1–2, 5; 9.1). That they were liberal Jewish Christians is suggested by Jerome's remark in his commentary on Isaiah 9:1 that the Nazoraeans interpret this passage as fulfilled by the mission of Paul and the inclusion of the whole world in the church. In an earlier comment on Isaiah 1:12 Jerome refers to friends of the Ebionites who maintain that the law must be kept only by Jews. If this is a reference to the Nazoraeans, it makes their liberal position clear. On the other hand Augustine several times refers to the Nazoraeans (*On Baptism* 7.1.1; *Against Cresconius* 1.31.36; *On*

Heresies 9) and once suggests that they were conservative Jewish Christians (*Against Faustus* 19.17). Jerome's information may be the more reliable because he seems to have had access to Nazoraean writings: an interpretation of Isaiah and a gospel, the latter of which is also mentioned by Epiphanius (*Against Heresies* 29.9.4). According to Epiphanius, the Nazoraeans were descendants of the Jerusalem church which fled to Pella at the time of the first Jewish war and from there went to Chochoba (29.7.7–8).

Decline of Liberal Jewish Christianity

The letters of Paul and Luke-Acts together make up more than half of the New Testament. However, despite this substantial representation of liberal Jewish Christians in early Christianity, this group seems to have faded fairly quickly from the early church. This disappearance was due to several factors; among them we may include the practical difficulty of combining Jewish and Gentile Christians in a single community, the fact that few Jews became Christians, the victory of the Romans over the Jews in the rebellions of 66 and 132 CE, and the adoption of arguments against Gentile Christian adherence to the law by Gentile Christians. We will consider each of these factors in turn.

As we have seen, both Paul and Luke-Acts advocate freedom from the law for Gentile Christians and see the union of Jewish and Gentile Christians in the church as an ideal. But this created a practical problem: how could law-abiding Jewish Christians live with the Gentile Christians who were not bound by the Jewish law? If the two were to live together, either the Gentiles would have to adopt part of the Jewish law or the Jews would have to abandon it partially. It is clear that both Paul and Luke-Acts advocate the latter solution. In Galatians 2:12 Paul refers to Peter's (and implicitly his and Barnabas') eating with Gentile Christians in Antioch. And in the story of the conversion of Cornelius in Acts 10:1–11:18 the problem of Peter's staying with him and eating with him (10:28; 11:3) is resolved by a vision in which Peter is told not to call unclean what God has called clean (10:11–16; 11:5–10). In context this probably means not abolition of the law, but rather relaxation of it to allow Jew and Gentile to live together as Christians. The four laws which Gentile Christians are to keep according to Luke, including abstinence from what is strangled and from blood, would make this easier.

Not all of the liberal Jewish Christians took this approach. As Paul tells us in Gal 2:12–14, at first Peter and the other Jewish Christians ate with the Gentile Christians in Antioch. But when some people arrived from James and the community in Jerusalem, Peter and Barnabas stopped eating with the Gentiles. Paul accused them of hypocrisy and of compelling the Gentile Christians to keep the law in effect if not intent. It seems unlikely that James, Peter and Barnabas were advocating that Gentile Christians partially keep the Jewish law; rather, they probably thought that the Jewish and Gentile Christians in Antioch should form separate communities. Since Paul does not report that his view prevailed, it seems likely that from that time on, the Jewish and Gentile Christians did not eat together in Antioch.

There is some indication that this was also a problem elsewhere. According to some interpreters, Rom 14–15 (and less directly the rest of the letter) is an attempt to unite communities of Jewish and Gentile Christians which are at odds. Here Paul argues that the strong, i.e., those who recognize that they are free with respect to the law, should not despise the weak. It is impossible to know the full dimensions of this problem, but it is likely that in many places

Jewish and Gentile Christians formed separate communities because of it.

The second factor is the lack of Jewish conversion to Christianity. It is again difficult to estimate the dimensions of this. But it is clear from Rom 9–11 that Paul is concerned by the failure of Jews to accept Christ. And that the number of Christian Jews is small is suggested by his reference to them as a remnant (11:5). Just before this he has quoted 1 Kings 19:18 with its reference to a remnant of seven thousand in the time of Elijah (11:4), but it is doubtful that he is thinking of this as the number of Christian Jews. Luke-Acts is concerned to emphasize the large number of Jews who have believed. This is clearest in Acts 21:20 which refers to myriads of Jewish believers in Jerusalem. But this is probably tendentious, an argument against the already emerging view that the Jews as a whole have rejected Jesus. Justin Martyr says that Christians from among the Gentiles are both more numerous and more true than those from among the Jews and Samaritans (*Apology* 53).

These two factors, taken together, mean that fairly early in the history of the liberal branch of the church, the Jewish Christians were small, isolated groups, outnumbered by the Gentile Christians. The Roman conquest of the Jews in 70 and 135 CE further exacerbated this situation. For one thing, this encouraged the Gentile Christians to separate themselves from Jews in order to avoid the wrath of Rome. And the reorganization of Judaism after 70 included, as we have seen, separation of itself from Christianity. Most importantly, however, the unsettled situation in Palestine weakened the most prestigious and influential liberal Jewish Christian community, i.e., the church in Jerusalem.

Josephus (*Antiquities* 20.200) and Hegesippus (in Eusebius, *Church History* 2.23) both report that shortly before the first Jewish revolt the leaders of the Jews in Jerusalem executed James, the brother of the Lord, then the leader of the Jerusalem church. Perhaps because of this, Eusebius (3.5) records that before the destruction of Jerusalem in 70, the Christian community fled to Pella, a town across the Jordan river. Following the destruction of Jerusalem, the community must have returned to the city since Eusebius lists fifteen bishops of Jerusalem who were of the circumcision, extending up to the time of the second rebellion (4.5). After the second rebellion, the bishop of Jerusalem was a Gentile and the church made up of Gentiles (4.6).

According to Justin Martyr (*Apology* 31) at the time of the second revolt, Bar Cochba, the leader of the revolution, threatened the Christians with punishment if they would not deny Jesus, presumably because faith in Jesus prevented recognition of Bar Cochba himself as messiah. In between the two rebellions Hegesippus also records an investigation by the emperor Domitian into two grandsons of Judas, the brother of the Lord (in Eusebius, *Church History* 3.20), and the execution under the emperor Trajan of Symeon, son of Clopas, who had succeeded James as leader of the Jerusalem church (3.32). Both actions may have been due to a desire to prevent further unrest in Judea.

The final factor in the decline of liberal Jewish Christianity is simply that Gentiles took up the arguments against Gentile Christians' keeping of the Jewish law. This was necessary because of the continuing attractiveness of Judaism for Gentile Christians. But arguments against keeping the law had one flavor as spoken by Jews and another as spoken by Gentiles. The unspoken context of the arguments made them different. For example, even Paul who takes a very critical stance vis-à-vis the law, could say in Rom 9:3–5:

> I could wish that I myself were accursed and cut
> off from Christ for the sake of my brethren, my
> kinsmen by race. They are Israelites and to them
> belong the sonship, the glory, the covenants, the
> giving of the law, the worship and the promises;
> to them belong the patriarchs, and of their race,
> according to the flesh, is the Christ.

For Paul all of this is obvious, but not so for Gentiles. To
Gentiles Paul's arguments against insisting that Gentile
Christians keep the Jewish law might easily have seemed
to be arguments against Jewish Christians' keeping of the
law, and ultimately against Judaism itself.

Similarly, those conservative Jewish Christian writings which were used by the liberal church, especially Matthew and John, with their harsh polemic against
unbelieving Israel, could easily have been understood by
Gentile Christians as critique of Jewish Christians as well
as Israel.

This is especially the case because insofar as the liberal
Jewish Christians were isolated from Gentile Christians,
they would tend to resemble the conservative Jewish
Christians. The two would differ theologically, but this difference would be manifest chiefly if they were in union
with Gentile Christians.

In his *Dialogue with Trypho* Justin Martyr tells us that in
his day there were some who ostracized liberal Jewish
Christians, but Justin himself thinks that they will be
saved, though he considers their observance of the law a
result of weak-mindedness (*Dial.* 47). Justin lacks any appreciation of the positive place of the people of Israel in the
Christian church, though he is tolerant of it. Before long,
even this tolerance ceases, as we shall see.

Summary

The earliest exponents of the view that Gentile Christians need not keep the Jewish law were themselves Jews— Paul, the author of Luke-Acts, possibly the author of Hebrews. Because of this, even though their position entailed a radical reevaluation of Judaism, which ultimately forced the separation of Christianity from Judaism, they retained a positive attitude toward Judaism. Luke-Acts sees it as legitimate for Jewish Christians to continue to observe the law. And Paul, even if he would not have agreed to this, retained a lively sense of the importance of the Jewish people in God's plan of salvation.

Such liberal Christians continued to exist for some time (e.g., especially the Nazoraeans). But rather early they became a minority in a church dominated by Gentile Christians. The reasons for this include the practical difficulties of combining Jewish and Gentile Christians in one community, lack of Jewish conversions to Christianity, the Roman conquests of Judea in 70 and 135 CE, and the adoption of arguments against Gentile Christian adherence to the law by Gentile Christians.

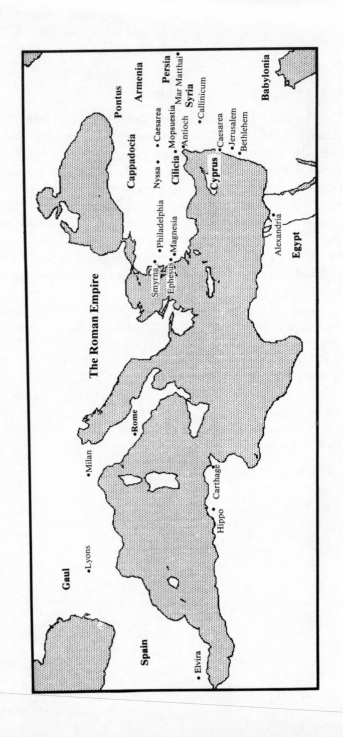

V.

LIBERAL GENTILE CHRISTIANITY

That eventually the liberal branch of the church was composed entirely of Gentiles who developed a negative view of Jewish Christianity and Judaism; at this point the separation of Christianity from Judaism was complete and Christianity became anti-Jewish.

Introduction

The use by Gentiles of arguments against Gentile Christians' keeping of the Jewish law tended, as we have already noted, to be less nuanced than Jewish use of such arguments. In the hands of Gentiles they easily became arguments against anyone's keeping the Jewish law, including Jewish Christians and Jews themselves. With the decline of liberal Jewish Christianity, this eventually became the position of liberal Christianity itself. This process extended over several centuries and involved factors in addition to the Gentilization of Christianity, as we shall see. But when it was complete, so was the emergence of Christianity from Judaism, and the stage was set for Christian anti-Judaism.

The only first century example of the undiscriminating

use by a Gentile of arguments against Gentile Christians' keeping of the law is the gospel of Mark, written either in Rome or Syria. In the second century we find examples of this in the letters of Ignatius of Antioch, written as he traveled through Asia Minor, and in the letter of Barnabas, perhaps deriving from Alexandria. In the third century the Didascalia, probably written in Syria, exemplifies this. Fourth century examples include the condemnation of the Nazoraeans as heretics by Epiphanius in Cyprus and Augustine in North Africa, the correspondence between Augustine and Jerome, then living in Bethlehem, and the homilies of John Chrysostom in Antioch.

Although their adoption by Gentiles was probably the main cause of the generalization of arguments against Gentile Christians' adherence to the law to apply to Jewish Christians and Jews, other factors were also significant. One such factor was the need to answer Jewish criticism of Gentile Christians for not keeping the Jewish law. The earliest example of such an answer to Jewish arguments is Justin Martyr's second century *Dialogue with Trypho*. This was written in Rome, but may reflect an actual dialogue in Ephesus. Similar responses were written in the third century in North Africa, Rome, Egypt and Caesarea, and in the fourth century in Syria and North Africa.

A second additional factor in the generalization of arguments against keeping the Jewish law was the need to refute Marcion, the Gnostics and the Manichaeans. Such refutations appeared in the second century in Rome and Lyons, in the third century in North Africa and at Caesarea, and in the fourth century in North Africa.

A third additional factor in the generalization of arguments against keeping the Jewish law was the need to respond to pagan criticism of Gentile Christians for not keeping it. Such responses began to appear in Rome in the second century, and later were written in North Africa and Caesarea in the third century, Caesarea in the fourth century, and Alexandria in the fifth century.

All of these additional factors were a result of the growth of the church especially among Gentiles. The decline of liberal Jewish Christianity opened the church to the charge of having abandoned the Jewish law. It may also have made easier the development of an extreme rejection of the law on the part of Marcion, the Gnostics and the Manichaeans. And the growth of the church and its increasing influence within the Roman empire gave rise to pagan criticism of Christianity. This reached its height in the short-lived attempt of the emperor Julian (361–3) to restore the eminence of pagan religion.

In focusing on the development of the liberal Gentile Christian attitude toward the Jewish law, we will ignore much of what preoccupied Christianity at this time. Internally this was a time of great theological ferment, generating disputes which frequently split the church. We will take some notice of the controversy over Gnosticism in its various forms, which extended from the second through the fourth century. Another devisive issue was the controversy over Arianism which raged through the fourth century. Arius proposed an understanding of the relationship between Jesus and the Father which was attractive to some and extremely repugnant to others. The views of Arius were rejected at the Council of Nicea in 325, but this did not end the controversy.

Externally this was a time during which Christianity was frequently persecuted by the Roman empire. And after the acceptance of Christianity during the reign of Constantine (305–37), the Roman emperors were increasingly involved in church affairs. As a result of the development of a theoretical anti-Judaism by the liberal Gentile

Christian church, the social position of the Jews suffered. During the fourth century the Jews steadily lost legal rights. For example, in 339 it became a crime to convert to Judaism (Codex Theodosianus 16.8.1). At the same time there were outbreaks of mob violence directed against the Jews. The most famous case occurred in 388. After a synagogue in Callinicum was destroyed, Ambrose, bishop of Milan (373–97), intervened to prevent the emperor Theodosius (379–95) from ordering the local bishop to rebuild the synagogue, or even from rebuilding it at the emperor's own expense (Letters, 40, 41). Unhappily, this was only the beginning of a long history of Christian anti-Judaism.

Our knowledge of the Roman empire during this period derives from Josephus, Tacitus, Suetonius and Dio Cassius; our knowledge of the Christian church derives chiefly from Eusebius.

We learn about liberal Gentile Christianity from the following sources:

1ST CENTURY—Gospel of Mark
probably a product of a liberal Gentile Christian community, in Rome or Syria in about 70

2ND CENTURY—Letters of Ignatius of Antioch
Ignatius presents the liberal Gentile Christian position in *Magnesians; Philadelphians*

Letter of Barnabas
presents the liberal Gentile Christian position

Justin Martyr
presents the liberal Gentile Christian position in *Apology; Dialogue with Trypho*

Letter to Diognetus
an apologetic presentation of Christianity which states the liberal Gentile Christian position on Judaism; author, place and exact time of composition unknown

Irenaeus
presents the liberal Gentile Christian position in *Against Heresies*

3RD CENTURY—Tertullian
presents the liberal Gentile Christian position in several writings

Hippolytus
presents the liberal Gentile Christian position in *Demonstration to the Jews*

Dialogue between Timothy and Aquila
presents the liberal Gentile Christian position; probably written in Egypt in about 200

Origen
presents the liberal Gentile Christian position in *On First Principles; Against Celsus*

Didascalia
presents the liberal Gentile Christian position

Cyprian (200–58)
born in Carthage in North Africa, he became a Christian in 246 and bishop of Carthage in 248; he was martyred in the persecution of the emperor Valerian (253–260); he pre-

sents the liberal Gentile Christian position in *Testimonies to Quirinius*

Novatian (210–80)

a convert to Christianity, he was ordained a presbyter in Rome; when Cornelius became pope in 251, Novatian became anti-pope and head of a rigorist church which endured for several centuries; he presents the liberal Gentile Christian position in *On Jewish Foods*

4TH CENTURY—Eusebius

presents the liberal Gentile Christian position in *Preparation for the Gospel; Demonstration of the Gospel*

Aphrahat (290–350)

born on the border of Persia and Syria, he became a Christian and, later, bishop of the monastery of Mar Matthai; he presents the liberal Gentile Christian position in his *Demonstrations*

Athanasius (297–373)

born in Alexandria, he became its bishop in 327; many times he was forced into exile or hiding by the Arians, whom he opposed; he presents the liberal Gentile Christian position in *On the Incarnation*

Epiphanius

presents the liberal Gentile Christian position in *Against Heresies*

Cyril of Jerusalem (315–86)

born in Jerusalem, he became its bishop in 349; like Athanasius he was several times expelled from his office by the

Arians; he presents the liberal Gentile Christian position in his catechetical works

Basil
presents the liberal Gentile Christian position in *Hexameron*

Gregory of Nyssa (330–95)
born in Caesarea in Cappadocia, brother of Basil, he became bishop of Nyssa in Armenia in 372; he presents the liberal Gentile Christian position in his catechetical works

Jerome
presents the liberal Gentile Christian position in his letters to Augustine

John Chrysostom
presents the liberal Gentile Christian position in his homilies against conservative Jewish Christianity

Theodore of Mopsuestia (350–428)
born in Antioch, he became bishop of Mopsuestia in Cilicia in 392; he presents the liberal Gentile Christian position in his catechetical homilies

Augustine
presents the liberal Gentile Christian position in several writings

5TH CENTURY—Cyril of Alexandria (376–444)
born in Alexandria, he became its bishop in 412; he presents the liberal Gentile Christian position in his homilies and in *Against Julian*

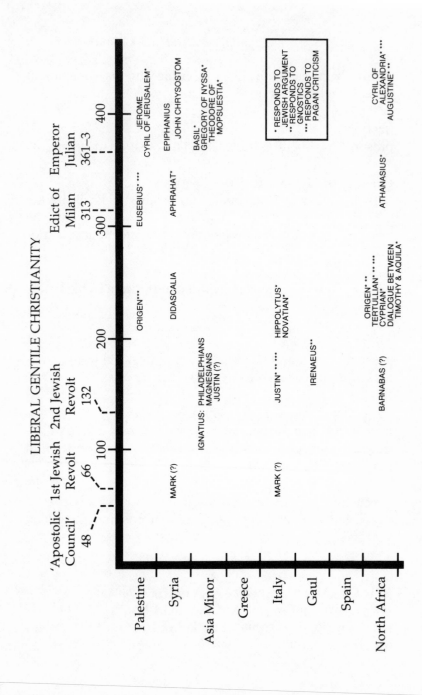

LIBERAL GENTILE CHRISTIANITY

	'Apostolic Council'	1st Jewish Revolt	2nd Jewish Revolt			Edict of Milan		Emperor Julian	
	48	66 100	132	200	300	313	361–3	400

Palestine — ORIGEN*** — EUSEBIUS* *** — JEROME / CYRIL OF JERUSALEM*

Syria — MARK (?) — DIDASCALIA — APHRAHAT* — EPIPHANIUS / JOHN CHRYSOSTOM — BASIL* / GREGORY OF NYSSA* / THEODORE OF MOPSUESTIA*

Asia Minor — IGNATIUS: PHILADELPHIANS / MAGNESIANS / JUSTIN (?)

Greece

Italy — MARK (?) — JUSTIN* *** — HIPPOLYTUS* / NOVATIAN*

Gaul — IRENAEUS**

Spain

North Africa — BARNABAS (?) — ORIGEN* ** / TERTULLIAN* / CYPRIAN* / DIALOGUE BETWEEN TIMOTHY & AQUILA* — ATHANASIUS* — CYRIL OF ALEXANDRIA* *** / AUGUSTINE* ***

* RESPONDS TO JEWISH ARGUMENT
** RESPONDS TO GNOSTICS
*** RESPONDS TO PAGAN CRITICISM

Gospel of Mark

The gospel of Mark is probably the earliest example of the presentation of the liberal position by a Gentile. It is of course not completely clear either that Mark was written by a Gentile or that it advocates a liberal position, but both seem probable. The strongest indication of this is to be seen in Mark 7:1–23. After mentioning in v 2 that the disciples of Jesus ate with unwashed hands, the author explains the Pharasaic and generally Jewish practice of washing hands and performing other sorts of purifications in v 3–4. The explanation clearly presupposes an audience unfamiliar with this Jewish practice, i.e., Gentiles; but the way the explanation is made also seems to distance the author from Judaism: he writes about *their* practice, not *our* practice. This suggests that the author is a Gentile.

A later authorial comment interprets Jesus' defense of his disciples for not washing their hands as a rejection of the law. Jesus defends them first by suggesting that this custom is a human tradition rather than a commandment of God (v 6–13) and then by arguing that nothing coming from outside a person can defile, but only that which comes from within (v 15, 18–19). Though the latter might have some sweeping implications, in context it may only be an argument that his disciples need not observe the practices of purification. But the author interprets: *Thus he declared all foods clean* (v 19). For Mark Jesus is not only defending his disciples for not washing their hands, but also sweeping away all of the legislation in the Hebrew scriptures about clean and unclean foods. This may also be implied for Mark in the story of Jesus' eating with tax collectors and sinners (2:15–17).

Perhaps Mark regards even the written laws concerning clean and unclean foods as human rather than divine.

He explicitly takes this position with respect to divorce in 10:2–9. There Jesus says that the law's permission of divorce comes from Moses, not from God. Perhaps Mark is suggesting something similar about the sabbath when he has Jesus say in 2:27 that the sabbath was made for human beings, not human beings for the sabbath. It seems clear from stories such as those found in 2:23–3:6 that Mark considers the sabbath law altered by Jesus.

Mark clearly affirms the ten commandments (10:17–22; 7:10) and the two great commandments (12:28–34) and does not make negative comments on any other part of the law (unless the scribe's elevation of love of neighbor above sacrifices in 12:33 is so construed). Still the impression given by the passages discussed above is that Jesus has ended the binding character of the Jewish law generally, with the exception of the ten commandments and the two great commandments. If that is correct, then Mark is quite similar to the other liberal Gentile Christians we will consider.

Ignatius of Antioch

If the above analysis is correct, then Mark is the earliest extant example of a liberal Gentile Christian point of view, coming from the time when the great examples of liberal Jewish Christianity, namely the letters of Paul and Luke-Acts, were being produced. Perhaps for this reason Mark does not yet clearly exhibit the use of this point of view against liberal Jewish Christians and against Israel itself, which is later characteristic of liberal Gentile Christianity. We can perhaps already see the beginning of this in the letters of Ignatius of Antioch. Although Ignatius, like Paul and Luke, sees the church as consisting ideally of Jew and Gentile (Smyr 1.2), and he does seem to refer positively to liberal Jewish Christians in Philad 6.1 as we have noted, his critique of conservative Jewish Christianity is not very discriminating. In Magn 8.1 he says that to live according to Judaism is to confess not having received grace, and in 10.3 that it is monstrous to talk of Jesus Christ and practice Judaism. Statements like these could be turned against liberal Jewish Christians as well as against conservatives. The same is true of Paul's arguments against conservative Jewish Christianity, but Paul's arguments are balanced by positive statements about the place of Israel in the plan of salvation, and Ignatius' are not. In Magn 9.1 Ignatius says that those who walked in ancient customs, i.e., the divine prophets (cf. 8.2), no longer kept the sabbath after they came to a new hope, i.e., in Christ. This may indicate that Ignatius himself would extend his critique of conservative Jewish Christians to apply to liberal Jewish Christians and Jews. In Philad 6.1 he says that unless they speak of Jesus Christ, both circumcision and uncircumcision are tombstones and sepulchres of the dead.

Letter of Barnabas

The author of the letter of Barnabas opposes the inclination of some of his readers to take upon themselves the Jewish law, by arguing that God's covenant with Israel came to an end when they sinned by worshiping the golden calf (cf. Exod 32). Consequently, Christians do not participate in God's covenant with Israel; rather, the covenant belongs to Christians alone, since the Jews lost it when Moses broke the tablets of stone after the people's sin with the golden calf (4.6–8; 13–14). And when the covenant with Israel came to an end, the literal sense of the law

was abolished; thereafter the law had properly only a figurative sense. Thus, for example, from that time on literal
sacrifice was abolished, and what was required was praise
(2.4–10). The author provides similar figurative interpre-
tations of fasting (3), circumcision (9), and the food laws
(10). He also interprets the ritual of the Day of Atonement
(7) and the sacrifice of the red heifer (8) as types of Jesus,
the sabbath as a type of eschatological rest at the end of
time (15) and the temple as a type of the church (16).

This was announced by the prophets, but the Jews
failed to understand it because of the influence of an evil
angel (9.4) or of the lusts of the flesh (10.9). Christians are
able to understand it only because the Lord planted wisdom and understanding (6.10) or teaching (9.9) in them,
because he circumcised their hearing (9.3). But it is still
possible for the evil one to enter them and hurl them from
life (2.10), which is the possibility against which the author
warns them.

This argument against conservative Jewish Christianity depends on denying the validity of Judaism after the
time of the sin with the golden calf. An argument of this
sort would come naturally only to a Gentile Christian, and
one who was not part of a church which included Jewish
Christians. For Barnabas Judaism and Christianity are almost completely separate.

Letter to Diognetus

An even greater degree of separation between Judaism and Christianity is manifested by this document,
whose author, date and place of origin are all uncertain. In
explaining why Christians do not keep the customs of the
Jews, the author first explains that Jewish sacrifices fool-

ishly presuppose that God is in need of the things which are sacrificed (4). He then criticizes the food laws as making an improper division between some created things and others, the sabbath law as forbidding good deeds on one day of the week, circumcision as mutilation of the flesh, and the festal calendar as a matter of arbitrary distinctions between days and seasons (5). Such a way of justifying Gentile Christian non-observance of the law implicitly denies the validity of its observance by Jewish Christians and Jews as well.

Didascalia

The Didascalia is a third century document, probably composed in Syria, which is concerned, especially in its final chapter, to dissuade its readers from adherence to the Jewish law. At several points the author speaks as though he is a Jewish Christian (cf. pp 164, 226, 228 in R. H. Connolly's translation), but since the Didascalia purports to be the work of the twelve apostles, who were Jewish Christians, it is not clear that this is reliable information about the actual author and not part of the fiction of apostolic authorship. The nature of the argument against the law makes it seem likely that the author is a Gentile.

The author several times suggests that he is addressing Gentiles (pp 164, 228), and it is clear that his argument against keeping the law does apply to Gentiles. But he seems most concerned to argue that Jewish Christians not keep the law. This is most explicit where he says that Jesus abolished the law and that he "did not say (this) to the Gentiles, but He said it to us His disciples from among the Jews, and brought us out from burdens and a heavy load" (p 226). That his argument is addressed to Jewish Christians is also indicated elsewhere (pp 216, 233; on pp 184–86 both Jewish and Gentile Christians are addressed).

The argument against keeping the Jewish law in the Didascalia is similar to that of the letter of Barnabas. The author divides the law into two parts: the first he simply calls the law; the second he calls the second legislation (pp 228–30). The first part of the law is that which is compatible with the gospel, specifically the ten commandments and the judgments (p 14). The second legislation consists of the remainder of the law, especially such things as sacrifice, purification, vows, the sabbath, the showbread, tithes, and first fruits (p 98). It is the second legislation which the author argues that his readers should not keep. In his view it was imposed by God as a punishment for Israel's sin in worshiping the golden calf (pp 12–14, 218–22, 224, 225, 230, 232). This second legislation punishes them not only by putting them in bondage, but also by blinding them to the advent of the savior.

According to the author the savior came to fulfill the law and to abolish the second legislation (p 14), thus making known the distinction between them. He sees Jesus' abolition of the second legislation indicated by the saying in Matt 11:28: 'Come to me all who labor and are heavy burdened, and I will give you rest' (pp 14, 98, 226). Secondly, he argues on p 226 that Jesus signified the abolition of the second legislation by not making use of any of the practices it commands. And thirdly, passages in the Hebrew scriptures themselves support the idea that Jesus has abolished the second legislation, in a variety of ways (cf. p 98).

In addition to the argument that Jesus abolished the second legislation, the author has two other general arguments against it. First, he argues that evil consequences result from keeping it. In particular he argues that those who keep the second legislation become guilty of the calf-worship on account of which it was imposed (p 232). Second, he says that Jesus not only abolished the second legislation in his own person, but also did so by means of the Romans (p 238). The Roman destruction of Jerusalem and complete political dominion over the Jews has made it impossible to keep the second legislation. The author also brings forward other arguments against particular laws. For example, he argues against observance of the sabbath by pointing out that every day is the Lord's (p 236).

Condemnation of the Nazoraeans as Heretics

The results of Gentiles' use of arguments against Gentile Christians' keeping of the Jewish law can be seen in their full flowering in the treatment of the Nazoraeans as heretics by Epiphanius (*Against Heresies* 29), who was himself a convert to Christianity from Judaism, and by Augustine (*On Heresies* 9). As we have seen, the Nazoraeans were probably liberal Jewish Christians. But from the point of view of Epiphanius and Augustine, there is no longer a significant difference between conservative and liberal Jewish Christians.

Correspondence between Augustine and Jerome

This development is illustrated in an illuminating way by the correspondence between Augustine and Jerome concerning the interpretation of Gal 2:11–14. In about 394 Augustine wrote from Hippo in North Africa to Jerome, who was then living in Bethlehem, in part to object to the interpretation of Gal 2:11–14 in Jerome's commentary on Galatians (Letter 28). Jerome had proposed that Paul's accusation that Peter compelled Gentiles to live like Jews (Gal

2:14) reflected Peter's polite pretense of doing so, not an actual error on the part of Peter. Augustine objected to the admission that there was any falsehood in scripture. In 397 Augustine sent a second letter raising the same question (Letter 40). In this letter Augustine explains further that Paul did not rebuke Peter for adhering to the Jewish law himself, something that Paul did and Peter could have done, provided that they did not consider observing the law necessary for salvation. Rather, Paul rebuked Peter for compelling Gentiles to observe the law, something absolutely forbidden. Augustine's concern here is the correct interpretation of scripture, especially the question of whether or not it contains falsehood. But in pursuit of this question he has accurately understood Paul's liberal Jewish Christian position as we have outlined it above.

Both of these letters from Augustine went astray, reaching Jerome indirectly. This caused hard feelings on Jerome's part which had to be soothed before he finally answered the question about Gal 2:11–14 in 404 (Letter 75). He answered by referring to other authorities who interpret the passage as he did and by proving from the Acts of the Apostles that Peter could not have believed that Gentiles needed to keep the Jewish law. Jerome refers to Augustine's idea that converted Jews, such as Paul and Peter, could keep the Jewish law, as a 'new argument.' He objects that to hold this is to fall into the heresy of Cerinthus and Ebion, and says that 'the ceremonies of the Jews are harmful and deadly to Christians, and . . . whoever keeps them, whether Jew or Gentile, is doomed to the abyss of the Devil.' He supports this by citing texts which speak of the end of the law, including Rom 10:4; Gal 5:2, 4, 18; 4:4, 5; 3:25; 4:1. Though Paul was arguing that Gentile Christians must not keep the Jewish law, Jerome understands him also to be prohibiting Jewish Christian observance of the law. An underlying presupposition is that it would be impossible to keep the law on any other basis than that it was necessary for salvation. Thus Jerome clearly reflects the then long-established use of arguments against Gentile Christians' keeping of the law in such a broad manner that they exclude liberal Jewish Christianity and Judaism itself.

Augustine, on the other hand, because of his careful exegesis, is aware of the nuances of Paul's argument. But that he shares Jerome's outlook becomes clear in his reply, written in 405 (Letter 82). Here he continues to argue for his interpretation of Gal 2:11–14, but makes it clear that he does not consider it proper at the present time for Jewish Christians to observe the Jewish law. Paul and others did so at first to prevent the observance of the law from being despised 'as if they were diabolic abominations.' But, argues Augustine, since they were types of future things, with the passing of time 'these observances were to be given up by all Christians.' And Augustine refers to his treatment of the point in his treatise *Against Faustus*. Thus Augustine ultimately represents the same view as Jerome, and differs only in that his exegesis of the scripture (in the service of showing it always truthful) compels him to see a development from the time of Paul to his own time.

Homilies of John Chrysostom

An even more extreme extension of the arguments against Gentile Christian observance of the Jewish law is visible in the homilies which John Chrysostom delivered in Antioch in 386–7. In these homilies he argues mainly that Christians should not participate in the synagogue worship of the Jews, as many were apparently doing. Chrysostom's goal was to persuade the members of his congregation to seek out and correct those who have been participating in Jewish worship; he ends each of the first seven homilies with an exhortation to do so, and the eighth homily is devoted almost entirely to such exhortation. But the principal content of the first seven homilies is argument against Christian participation in Jewish worship. Chrysostom intended his congregation to use these arguments against the Christians who were drawn to Jewish worship and was probably also trying to forestall any further defections to the synagogue.

Though the problem Chrysostom confronted arose from contact between his congregation and non-Christian Jews, rather than conservative Jewish Christians, it is closely parallel to the situation Paul addressed in several of his letters. And Chrysostom makes some use of Paul's counter-arguments, citing Gal 4:25–6 (1.4.7); 5:2 (2.1.4–2.2; 3.3.9; 8.5.5); 5:3 (2.2.2–4); 5:4 (2.2.1; 2.3.8; 6.7.4; 8.5.5); 2:21 (2.2.1); 4:12 (3.3.1–2); Rom 11:6 (2.2.1); and Phil 3:7 (3.3.2). For the most part in these passages Chrysostom correctly sees Paul as arguing that Gentile Christians should not keep the Jewish law. However, in 2.1.6–7 we can see that he also understands Gal 5:2 as a condemnation of Jews who did not forsake the law and turn to Christ. Similarly, in 1.2.1 he understands Rom 11:16–17 as a reference to the rejection of the Jews who crucified Jesus, overlooking the main thrust of Rom 11:17–24, namely, that Gentile Christians have been grafted into the people of Israel. And in 1.2.2 Chrysostom understands Phil 3:2–3, a passage which probably refers to conservative Jewish Christians, as an identification of Jews as dogs. Thus in Chrysostom we can clearly see the extension of arguments against Gentile Christian observance of the law to apply to Jewish observance of the law.

However, this is not Chrysostom's chief argument

against Jewish observance of the law. His most important argument is that because the Jews crucified Christ (6.2.10; 6.3.3; 6.4.5, 7; 6.5.4–5) God rejected them, destroying Jerusalem and the temple (1.4.2; 1.7.4; 3.3.6–7; 4.6.1, 6–9; 6.3.6–7; 6.4.1, 3–4; 6.7.4); since much of the law can only be kept in Jerusalem and the temple, all Jewish observances are now sins (3.5.7; 3.6.1; 4.3.8–9; 4.4.2–8; 4.7.4–7; 5.1.3, 5; 7.1.3–4; 7.2.1–2). In support of this he argues that the exiles in Babylon did not continue Jewish observances while they were away from Jerusalem and the temple (4.4.9–5.8; 5.1.4). God's rejection of Judaism was not a sudden change of plan, but was foreseen by the prophets (4.6.2–3; 5.9–10; 5.12.2–9; 6.2.1–3; 7.2.4–6.1). The law was a penultimate dispensation (2.2.5–8; 7.2.8), permitted because of Jewish weakness (4.6.4–5). Christ kept the law only to fulfill it (3.3.9–4.1).

In addition to arguments of this sort, Chrysostom also attempts to achieve his purpose by vilifying the Jews. His most frequent charges include descriptions of the synagogue as a den of thieves (1.3.1; 1.4.2; 5.12.12; 6.7.4–6) or a dwelling place of demons (1.3.1; 1.4.2; 1.6.2, 6–8; 1.7.5–11; 2.3.5; 5.12.12; 6.7.6). He supports these and other accusations by appealing to statements about the Jews in the Hebrew scriptures (e.g., 1.3.1). But above all, Chrysostom attacks the Jews as the slayers of Christ. Not only does he argue that God has rejected them because they killed Jesus, as we have noted; he also uses this to discredit Jews in the eyes of Christians (1.3.3; 1.4.5; 1.5.1; 1.6.3; 1.7.2, 5; 2.3.5, 8; 3.6.6; 4.3.6; 6.1.7; 6.7.4, 5; 8.5.4).

In these homilies we see the final results of the Gentilization of the church. In continuing the liberal Christian argument that Gentile Christians need not keep the Jewish law, Gentile Christians finally deny the legitimacy of Judaism itself and become harsh critics of the Jews.

Factors in Addition to the Gentilization of Christianity

Although adoption of arguments against keeping the law by Gentile Christians was probably the single most important cause of their being generalized to apply not only to Gentiles, but also to Jewish Christians and even Jews, there were several additional factors which promoted the same development. These include: Jewish arguments against Christian non-observance of the law, the extreme anti-nomianism of Marcion and the Gnostics, and pagan criticism of Christians for abandoning Judaism. We will discuss each of these in turn.

1. Jewish Arguments

As we have seen, throughout its early history Christianity had to contend with the attractiveness of Judaism for its Gentile converts. Beginning in the second century Jews also argued that Christians should keep the law. It is possible that such argument goes back even earlier. But it is clear that from the time such arguments began to be put forward, Christians had to answer them. And the need to answer them exacerbated the inclination of Gentile Christians to argue in return not only that Gentile Christians did not need to keep the law, but also that Christians generally did not need to keep it, and even that Jews should not. The earliest example of such an argument is Justin's *Dialogue with Trypho*.

Justin's *Dialogue with Trypho*

In this dialogue Justin responds to the Jewish argument, presented by Trypho, that Christians should keep the law. In response Justin divides the law into two categories: on the one hand, commands ordained for worship of God and the practice of righteousness; and on the other, injunctions referring to the mystery of Christ or given on account of Israel's hardness of heart (44.2; 45.3; 67.10). Justin accepts the first part of the law as binding on the Christian; to this extent he and Trypho share common ground. It is the rest of the law which Trypho argues that Christians should keep (8.4; 10; 19.1; 26.1; 46.2; 47.1) and which Justin argues against. Trypho summarizes this part of the law in 8.4: circumcision and keeping the sabbath, feasts and new moons. In 46.2 he adds ritual washing.

Justin's description of this second part of the law as injunctions referring to the mystery of Christ, or given on account of Israel's hardness of heart, also indicates his argument against it. Like the letter of Barnabas, Justin regards this part of the law as having a figurative meaning. For example, he argues that the paschal lamb is a prefigurement of Christ (40.1–3). However, unlike Barnabas, Justin also sees this part of the law as having a literal meaning, i.e., commandments given on account of Israel's hardness of heart. Justin seems to mean two things by this:

(a) the law was given as a sign setting the Jews apart so that they might suffer their present trials; this is especially true of circumcision (16.2; 19.2, 5; 23.4, 5; 92.2–3; 137.1), but also applies more generally (21.1); and

(b) the law was also given to oppose idolatry (19.6; 22.11; 27.2–3; 92.4), keeping the memory of God before their eyes (19.6; 20.1; 27.4; 46.5–6), thus remedying their spiritual disease (30.1); in 19.6 and 20.4 Justin says that the sin with the golden calf was the occasion for this legislation.

Justin's basic argument that the law should be divided thusly is that in Jesus the new covenant promised by the prophets has arrived, revealing this division of the law in two and showing the second category to consist of laws occasioned by Israel's hardness of heart (67.9–10). He did this by giving a new law, chiefly the commandments to love God and neighbor (93.2), which affirms that which is enduring in the old law and simultaneously reveals the part of the law given on account of Israel's hardness of heart. The Jews have failed to recognize Jesus as the fulfillment of prophecies, and so have failed to understand the true character of the law, because God has withheld from them the ability to discern the wisdom of the scriptures on account of their wickedness (55.3).

In addition to this basic argument, Justin presents many other arguments to show that specific parts of the law are references to the mystery of Christ or were given on account of Israel's hardness of heart, and thus are not binding on the Christian. For example, in 40 Justin argues that the rituals of Passover and the Day of Atonement were types of Christ because both can be celebrated only in Jerusalem, which has been given over to the enemies of the Jews. In 46.2 Trypho agrees that this makes the entire sacrificial cult impossible. Elsewhere Justin argues that to presume the literal validity of his second category of laws either leads one to speak inappropriately about God or implies that he is inconsistent. Thus in 22.1, 11 and 67.8 Justin argues that God has no need of sacrifice. And in 23.1–5 he supports his case by arguing that the patriarchs were righteous without keeping the law, and by arguing that women are righteous without being circumcised.

Like Barnabas Justin argues against the law without rejecting or criticizing God by taking a rather negative view of Judaism, seeing a great part of the law as necessary because of the faults of the Jews. As we have already seen, in 47 Justin mentions liberal Jewish Christians and says that unlike some others, he is willing to tolerate them. But it is clear that his perspective on the law can allow for no positive view of Jewish Christianity or Judaism itself; his tolerance is simply a concession to their weakness.

After the time of Justin similar arguments in response to Jewish argumentation that Christians should keep the law continued to be made for centuries. Tertullian wrote a treatise *Against the Jews;* and Hippolytus wrote a *Demonstration to the Jews,* of which only a fragment survives. A *Dialogue between Timothy and Aquila,* a Jew, seems to have been written in Egypt in about 200 CE. Origen mentions Jewish argument that the law must be understood literally and uses the impossibility of keeping the sabbath and the dietary laws to show that they must be understood allegorically (*On First Principles* 4.3.2). He also argues against the Jewish literal interpretation of circumcision (*Homilies on Genesis* 3.4–6; *on Romans* 2.13) and argues that Passover cannot be observed because the temple has been destroyed (*Homilies on Romans* 2.13). Cyprian (200–258), bishop of Carthage c. 248–58, argued in his *Testimonies to Quirinius* that the Jews had been replaced by the Christians. In three letters to his congregation in Rome (of which only *On Jewish Foods* survives) the anti-pope Novatian (210–80) argued that the Jews do not understand their own law because they fail to see that the law is spiritual. Eusebius addressed his *Demonstration of the Gospel* to the Jews, explaining why Christians do not keep the biblical law. Aphrahat (c. 290–350) responded to Jewish criticism of Syrian Christianity in his *Demonstrations*. And Augustine also wrote a *Tractate against the Jews*. To works like these which directly respond to Jewish argument against Christianity, we may add many others which recognize that Jews and Greeks raise different questions about Christianity and must be answered differently. In this category we find the catechetical works of Gregory of Nyssa (330–395), Cyril of Jerusalem (315–386) and Theodore of Mopsuestia (350–428), Athanasius' (297–373) treatise *On the Incarnation*, the *Hexameron* of Basil (320–379) and the homilies of Cyril of Alexandria (376–444). Rosemary Radford Ruether has analyzed these responses to Jewish argument against Christians as focusing on two themes. First, they argue that in its literal sense the law had a negative purpose and that now it is properly to be understood spiritually. Second, they argue that the Jews have been rejected by God, while Gentile Christians have been elected.

2. Marcion and the Gnostics

In addition to Jewish argument against Christians, the extreme anti-nomianism of Marcion and the Gnostics also provided an impetus toward the generalization of arguments against the Jewish law to apply not only to Gentile Christians, but also to Jewish Christians and Jews. It did so because in order to answer the arguments against the law advanced by the Gnostics and Marcion, its defenders rejected much of the law, agreeing that it was imperfect, so as to save what they considered the essential elements of the law. Thus the argument against the Gnostic position was similar to the argument against conservative Jewish Christianity. This may explain the treatment of Gnostics and conservative Jewish Christians together by the heresiologists (e.g., Irenaeus, Hippolytus, Epiphanius).

It is not yet clear exactly when and how Gnosticism first appeared. Certainly in the second century of the

Common Era, various Gnostic groups existed, engaged in a missionary and theological struggle with non-Gnostic Christians. Gnosticism was an extremely varied phenomenon, but all its forms shared a family resemblance. One thing which many shared was an argument against the Jewish law. In a sense Gnosticism was more consistent than the liberal Gentile Christianity we are considering. If the law, given by God, was obsolete, at least to the extent that it was not required of Gentiles for salvation, then the god who gave the law must not be the true God. Thus the typical Gnostic position is that the law does not derive from the true, transcendent God, but rather from at best a subordinate deity, and at worst an enemy of the true God. Consequently the law has no validity for the Christian. Rather it is part of the created order which it is the goal of the Gnostic to escape in order that he may return to the true God from which creation separates him.

Those who held it supported this view of the law in various ways. Marcion, who differed from the Gnostics in other ways but had a view of the law similar to theirs, came from Pontus to Rome c. 150 CE. After separating from the church of Rome, he founded a church which lasted for several centuries. His extreme rejection of the law was inspired by Paul, but he argued his position in a different way than Paul had. He wrote a book called *Antitheses* in which he systematically contrasted the teaching of Jesus, representing the true, transcendent God, with the teaching of the Hebrew scriptures. For example, one of the antitheses states:

The Creator established the Sabbath; Christ abolishes it.

By means of an accumulation of such contrasts, Marcion supported his contention that the law was not given by the true God.

Letter of Ptolemy to Flora

Gnostic argumentation against the law is presented most extensively in a letter from Ptolemy, a student of the famous Gnostic teacher Valentinus, to an otherwise unknown person named Flora. In it Ptolemy explains the proper understanding of the law. This letter, which is preserved by Epiphanius, dates from mid-second century CE. Ptolemy begins by saying that he cannot accept the view of some that the law derives from the perfect God because it is imperfect and needs to be completed by another and because it includes commandments unsuited to such a God. Nor can he accept the view of others that the law derives from the devil, since it forbids injustice, and Jesus said that a house divided against itself cannot stand (*Against Heresies* 33.3.1–5). This initial observation that the law is a mixture of good and bad leads Ptolemy to his moderate Gnostic conclusion that this is because the law derives from the demiurge, the creator god, who is between the perfect God and the devil (33.7.3–4). But Ptolemy further supports and nuances his argument by maintaining that the law has three divisions: one part derives from the elders of the people, another from Moses, and only the third from god, i.e., the demiurge. This division is based on sayings of Jesus in Matt 15:4–9 (Jesus' charge that the Pharisees and scribes have voided the word of God for the sake of their tradition) and 19:3–8 (Jesus' statement that the permission of divorce derives from Moses) (33.4). Ptolemy then further divides the part of the law which does derive from god (= the demiurge) into three parts: the pure legislation (= the ten commandments) which the savior fulfills; a part mingled with evil and injustice (e.g., the law of talion) which the savior abolishes; and a typological or symbolic part (e.g., circumcision) which is abolished in its literal sense and has received a new spiritual application (33.5).

As I have already mentioned, the argument against the Marcionite and Gnostic position partly allowed the validity of the position, but explained why God had given that part of the law which was found objectionable, making it possible to avoid rejecting other elements of the law and the God who gave it. Thus the argument against this position was very similar to the argument against conservative Jewish Christianity; in both cases the same elements of the law were rejected. However, since the issue in the discussion with Marcion and the Gnostics was not that of keeping the law, but rather its theological evaluation, the argument against Marcion and the Gnostics was inevitably an argument against the validity of the law for anyone, not only Gentile Christians, but also Jewish Christians and Jews.

The earliest example of such an argument against Marcion and the Gnostics is the lost treatise of Justin Martyr against Marcion (cf. *Apology* 26). It has been argued that his *Dialogue with Trypho* reflects his arguments against Marcion. The earliest surviving argument is that of Irenaeus who opposes the Gnostics along with Marcion. In *Against Heresies* 4.12–19 he argues that Christ did not abrogate the natural precepts of the law, by which we are justified (4.13), but only the traditions of the elders which had been added to it (4.12) and that part of it which had been laid down for those in bondage (4.13, 15) which loses its force when Christ brings freedom (4.13). He further argues that

God had no need of the Jewish cult, but established it for the good of the Jews (4.17). Another example of such argument is found in Tertullian's treatise *Against Marcion*. Tertullian exculpates God from the deficiencies of the Jewish scripture by arguing that they were necessitated by the deficiencies of the Jews. And Origen, in *On First Principles* 4, responds not only to Jewish argument against Christianity, but also to the arguments of heretics who deny that the creator is God, i.e., Gnostics and Marcionites (cf. 4.2.1.). He argues that scripture must be interpreted allegorically.

Somewhat later Manicheism revived the extreme antinomianism of the Gnostics and Marcionites. Manicheism arose as a result of the preaching of Mani (216–275 CE) in Babylonia. Mani's religion was a highly syncretistic combination of Buddhism, Zoroastrianism and Christianity, which Hans Jonas has described as the most important product of Gnosticism. It included a view of the Hebrew scriptures very similar to that of Marcion. By the fourth century Manicheism was strong in north Africa. Augustine, who had earlier been a Manichean himself, devoted a number of writings to refutation of Manicheism. The most extensive of these is his treatise *Against Faustus*, a Manichean whom Augustine knew personally.

Faustus had argued that in order to be consistent, the Christians who do not keep the Jewish law must also reject the Hebrew scriptures in which it is found. Augustine's counter-argument is that the laws which Christians do not keep must be understood as symbols of what was to come (cf. 4, 8, 10 etc.). Depending on Rom 11, Augustine argues that Christians must retain the Hebrew scriptures in order to be grafted into the holy stock of the Hebrews (9), but he clearly presupposes that it is now illegitimate for anyone, including Jewish Christians and Jews, to observe literally the symbolic part of the law. In passing he remarks that the reason the Jews in the past had to observe literally what was intended as a prefigurement is that this was suited to their character (22.21).

3. Pagan Criticism of Christianity

A third factor which encouraged the generalization of arguments against keeping the Jewish law to include both Jewish Christians and Jews was pagan criticism of Christianity for its abandonment of Judaism. This presented the same problem as did the Jewish criticism we have already discussed; it simply came now from a different quarter. In this case too, the attempt to defend Christian non-observance of the law easily lost the nuance provided by Paul and Luke-Acts, and became a general rejection of the continuing validity of Judaism for anyone.

This sort of pagan criticism of Christianity is implied by the response made to it both by Justin Martyr in his *Apology* and by Tertullian in his *Apology*. Both writers attempt to claim the Jewish past for Christianity, arguing that Christians and not Jews have the correct understanding of the Jewish scriptures (Justin; cf. *Apology* 31, 36, 49, 53, 63), and that God has rejected Jews in favor of Christians, as the Jews' expulsion from Palestine shows (Tertullian; cf. *Apology* 21, 26).

The first pagan critic whose name we know was Celsus. As we have already noted, in his *True Doctrine* Celsus argued (among other things) that Christians were apostates from Judaism. Origen's *Against Celsus* is a long refutation of this and the other arguments of Celsus. Celsus apparently made this charge by introducing into his work as a character a Jew who accused Christian converts from

Judaism of abandoning the law. Thus Celsus made his point by taking up the Jewish argument against Christianity. Origen's response is twofold. He first denies that Jewish Christians have abandoned the law, citing the Ebionites and the presentation of Peter in the New Testament (*Against Celsus* 2.1). However, this seems to be mainly a debating point. Origen's more substantial response is that as Jesus promised, the Holy Spirit has been given to Christians to reveal to them the allegorical meaning of the Hebrew scriptures (2.2–4). Later Celsus makes his argument in a different way. He says that since they disagree with one another, either Moses or Jesus must have taught falsely, or God forgot or changed his mind between the time of Moses and the time of Jesus. Here Celsus takes up (whether consciously or not) the arguments of Marcion and the Gnostics. Once again Origen answers by saying that the Hebrew scriptures must be interpreted allegorically (7.18). Thus, in responding to the criticism of Celsus, Origen takes up a position which not only allows for Gentile Christians not to keep the law, but also implies that Jewish Christians and Jews should not do so.

Other charges made by Celsus lead Origen to express an even more negative view of Judaism. For example, Celsus' Jew says that if Jesus were what Christians assert that he is, the Jews would not have rejected him. Origen replies that this rejection was foretold by the prophets and that as a consequence of it the Jews have been rejected by God, as their expulsion from Jerusalem shows (*Against Celsus* 2.8). Origen also appeals to this in answering the charge that those who condemned Jesus received no punishment (2.34; 4.22; 8.42). He even uses this view to defend pre-Christian Judaism against Celsus' attacks (4.32; 5.43; 7.8) and to justify God's treatment of the Jews (8.67).

Another pagan who criticized Christians for abandoning the Jewish law was the philosopher Porphyry (c. 233–302). In at least two works, *Philosophy from Oracles* and *Against the Christians*, Porphyry attacked Christianity for apostasy from Judaism, among other things. Eusebius answered this and the other arguments of Porphyry in his *Preparation for the Gospel* and *Demonstration of the Gospel*, two long apologetic works written c. 314–23. In the former Eusebius responds to this criticism only briefly and indirectly. He implies that Christianity is identical with the religion of the Hebrew patriarchs. It antedates Judaism, which was a temporary disposition to allow knowledge of the Hebrew scriptures to circulate so that all could embrace the religion of the patriarchs revealed fully and to all in Christianity (*Preparation* 7.6–8; 8.1). Thus Christianity is not apostasy from Judaism, but rather the revival of something older than Judaism, a revival which the Hebrew scriptures predicted. In book 1 of *Demonstration of the Gospel* Eusebius repeats this argument (1.2) in order to explain why Christians make use of the sacred writings of the Jews, but do not embrace their manner of life. He argues that the Mosaic law was not intended for all people, but can be kept only by Jews living in Palestine (1.3–4), and that it was given to counteract the ill-effects of the Israelites' sojourn in Egypt (1.4, 6). Christianity is the revival of the religion of the pre-Mosaic patriarchs which was predicted in the Hebrew scriptures (1.5–6). Christians do not practice polygamy and offer sacrifices as the pre-Mosaic patriarchs did, because now there is no need to increase population as there was then, and because the death of Christ has made other sacrifices unnecessary (1.9–10). Not only did the Hebrew scriptures foretell the revival of patriarchal religion in Christianity; they also predicted the destruction of Jerusalem and the dispersal of the Jews among the Gentiles (1.1).

Another pagan critic of Christianity was the emperor Julian (331–363). In his book *Against the Galileans* he used arguments like those of Celsus to say that Christians had illegitimately forsaken the Mosaic law. This argument was answered by Cyril of Alexandria in his work *Against Julian*, written about 440. Like Origen, Cyril argues that Christians have not abandoned the law, but simply interpret it properly, i.e., allegorically. Not only did Julian argue against Christianity; he also sought to weaken it by rebuilding the Jewish temple in Jerusalem, rendering Christian argument that Judaism had come to an end ineffective. The failure of this project had, naturally, exactly the opposite effect.

Summary

As Gentile Christians increasingly dominated the church, they became its spokesmen in presenting the arguments against Gentile Christians' keeping the Jewish law. But because they easily lost sight of the positive place of Judaism in the economy of salvation, they tended to generalize this position so that not only Gentile Christian but also Jewish Christian observance of the law was prohibited. And this was easily generalized further to become a condemnation of Judaism itself. This process can be seen in a series of writings beginning with the gospel of Mark and including the letters of Ignatius of Antioch, the letter of Barnabas, the letter to Diognetus, the Didascalia, the correspondence between Augustine and Jerome, and the homilies of John Chrysostom.

This adoption by Gentiles of arguments against the Jewish law was in itself probably the most important factor in generalizing these arguments so as to prohibit both liberal Jewish Christianity and Judaism itself. But there were other contributing factors, including the need to respond to Jewish arguments against Christianity, the anti-nomianism of Marcion, the Gnostics and the Manicheans, and pagan criticism of Christianity for apostatizing from Judaism.

CONCLUSION

We have seen that Christianity emerged from Judaism chiefly as a result of two things: first, the decision made by most of the church that Gentile Christians need not keep the Jewish law; and second, the adoption of this position by Gentile Christians, who understood it to mean that neither Jewish Christians nor Jews should keep the law. As we have noted, Jesus himself stood in some tension with the Judaism of his time, but perhaps no more so than some of the prophets. The belief that Jesus was the messiah, when it arose among some of the Jews, certainly set them apart from the rest of Israel which did not share this belief; but it is conceivable that the Christians might have remained a sect of Judaism if they had not admitted Gentiles to their company without requiring that they keep the law. This seems to be suggested by the fate of conservative Jewish Christianity which remained simultaneously a sect of Judaism and of liberal Christianity. Relations between conservative Jewish Christianity and Judaism might have been even more cordial if the crisis created by the failure of the Jewish revolutions of 66 and 132 had not forced Judaism to retrench.

The decision to admit Gentiles to the Christian church without requiring them to keep the law certainly distanced Christianity from Judaism. But this liberal Christianity might have had a more positive appreciation of Judaism, and better relations with it, if it had continued to include Jewish Christians. What finally divided Christianity from Judaism was the disappearance of liberal Jewish Christians and the inheritance of their theological position by Gentile

Christians. This in itself was the principal factor, but as we have seen, Jewish criticism of Christianity, the extreme anti-nomianism of Marcion and the Gnostics, and pagan criticism of Christianity were also contributory factors.

A survey of the history of the separation of Christianity from Judaism is interesting, I think, but, more importantly, offers the possibility of retrieving elements of the past for the present. There seems to be little possibility of retrieving the conservative stance; the decision that Gentiles need not keep the Jewish law was a conscious choice that has been reaffirmed again and again in the history of the church. However, the same cannot be said for the liberal Jewish Christian stance; its loss was almost accidental, the result of the replacement of liberal Jewish Christians with Gentiles who were not aware of their relationship, as Christians, to Judaism. The liberal Gentile Christians forgot that they had been grafted into the root of Judaism. This forgetfulness is strikingly illustrated by a comment made by Clement of Alexandria (died c. 215) in his *Miscellanies* (6.15). Clement interprets Rom 11:17 as a reference to the grafting of converts to Christianity into the Word. He distinguishes four types of converts which correspond to four ways in which a graft may be made. His second type of convert includes Gentiles who have studied philosophy and Jews; Clement considers the two to be approximately equal in their preparedness for Christianity. Clement's interpretation of the cultivated olive tree as the Word, and the wild olive tree as including Jews who need to be grafted into the Word, reverses Paul's use of the metaphor and shows to what extent the Jewish roots of Christianity have been forgotten. This is precisely what Paul was trying to prevent by using the image.

But since the loss of this liberal Jewish Christian stance was accidental, a matter of forgetting, it is conceivable that we retrieve this position for our time. One warrant for doing so is that liberal Jewish Christian writings have been accepted as normative for the Christian community. This may even mean that we must retrieve this position for to-day. If we did so, the first result would be a more positive attitude toward the people of Israel, the Jews. It is true that Paul and Luke-Acts present a critique of non-Christian Is-rael, and that Paul understands the law in a way that would not be acceptable to Jews. But this is combined with an awareness that the Jews, not only in the past but also now, are the people of God. Gentile Christians share in the salvation which God has accomplished for Israel through Jesus, but they do not replace Israel. To use Paul's figure, Gentiles have been grafted into the root of Israel (Rom 11:17–24); to use Luke's, they have become a people asso-ciated with the redeemed people of Israel (Acts 15:14–18). And if much of Israel has mysteriously not recognized God's salvation in Jesus, in the end, says Paul, all Israel will be saved (Rom 11:26). To have retained this positive ap-preciation of Israel might have prevented much Christian anti-Semitism in the past; to retrieve it for our time might put relations between Christians and Jews on a much bet-ter foundation than otherwise supports them.

In addition to improving relations between Christians and Jews, recovery of the outlook of Paul and Luke-Acts for our time would also suggest a different way of treating Jewish converts to Christianity than that we currently em-ploy. From the point of view of Paul and Luke-Acts, Jewish converts need not give up the practice of Judaism, and per-haps even should not. Jewish converts would be encour-aged to combine the observance of the law with belief in Christ, to remain Jewish Christians in the fullest sense. Eventually this might produce a significant number of such Jewish Christians as a part of the church. Paul, Luke-Acts and Ignatius of Antioch, as we have seen, consider such a union of Jew and Gentile in the church to be ideal. In the practical order, it seems likely that such a revival of Jewish Christianity is our best hope for an effective reduction of Christian anti-Semitism.

But if their presence in the New Testament would warrant reviving the views of Paul and Luke-Acts, what about the views of Matthew, John and James, which are also part of the New Testament? We may first of all note that they can be harmonized fairly easily with a liberal view, as must have been the opinion of those liberal Christians who took them into the canon. It is principally when these documents are read in isolation that their conservative stance becomes clear. Still they do speak more positively about the law than do the liberal writings of the New Testament. Interpreted in the context of the New Testament as a whole, their affirmation of the law can be seen as an affirmation of it for Jewish Christians or as an affirmation of its penultimate value. Or perhaps these conservative writings must be seen as modifying the complete freedom of Gentile Christians from the law which Paul and Luke-Acts advocate. The combination of liberal and conservative writings within the New Testament may imply that Gentile Christians should keep the law in some degree. This is a common conclusion, as we can see from the widespread view that the ten commandments are binding for Gentile Christians.

Within the Roman Catholic Church a significant step toward the retrieval of the liberal Jewish Christian view was taken in Vatican II's Declaration on the Relationship of the Church to Non-Christian Religions (*Nostra Aetate*) 4. Drawing upon Paul's letters to the Galatians and Romans, the Declaration notes that Gentile Christians have been grafted into the stock of Israel and that the Jews continue to be most dear to God, who does not repent of his call. Thus, the Roman Catholic Church has already officially endorsed the first of the consequences of retrieving the liberal Jewish Christian position, i.e., a new attitude toward Israel. Similar statements have been made by other Christian groups. Unfortunately, it is my impression that these statements have not yet had much impact on the Christian church at large.

BIBLIOGRAPHY

A. General

Brown, S., "The Matthean Community and the Gentile Mission," *NovT* 22 (1980) 193–221.

Dahl, N.A., *Das Volk Gottes: Eine Untersuchung zum Kirchenbewusstsein des Urchristentums*. Reprint. Darmstadt: Wissenschaftliche Buchgesellschaft, 1963 (original publication 1941).

Dix, G., *Jew and Greek: A Study in the Primitive Church*. London: Dacre, 1953.

Goppelt, L., *Christentum und Judentum in ersten und zweiten Jahrhundert*. Gütersloh: Bertelsmann, 1955.

Jocz, J., *The Jewish People and Jesus Christ: A Study in the Relationship Between the Jewish People and Jesus Christ*. London: SPCK, 1949.

Koenig, J., *Jews and Christians in Dialogue: New Testament Foundations*. Philadelphia: Westminster, 1979.

Meeks, W.A. and R.L. Wilken, *Jews and Christians in Antioch in the First Four Centuries of the Common Era*. Society of Biblical Literature Sources for Biblical Study, 13; Missoula, MT: Scholars, 1978.

Richardson, P., *Israel in the Apostolic Church*. SNTSMS 10; Cambridge: University Press, 1969.

Simon, M., *Verus Israel. Etude sur les relations entre chretiens et juifs dans l'empire romain* (135–425). Paris: E. de Boccard, 1964 (original publication 1948).

Wilde, R., *The Treatment of the Jews in the Greek Christian Writers of the First Three Centuries*. Washington: Catholic University of America Press, 1949.

B. Introduction

Baum, G., *Is the New Testament Anti-Semitic? A Re-examination of the New Testament.* Glen Rock, NJ: Paulist, 1965.

Davies, A. T., ed., *Anti-Semitism and the Foundations of Christianity.* New York: Paulist, 1979.

Gager, J., *The Origins of Anti-Semitism: Attitudes Toward Judaism in Pagan and Christian Antiquity.* New York: Oxford, 1983.

Idinopulos, T. A. and R. B. Ward, "Is Christianity Inherently Anti-Semitic? A Critical Review of Rosemary Ruether's *Faith and Fratricide,*" *JAAR* 45 (1977) 193–214.

Parkes, J., *The Conflict of the Church and the Synagogue: A Study in the Origins of Antisemitism.* New York: Athenaeum, 1974 (original publication 1934).

Ruether, R. R., *Faith and Fratricide: The Theological Roots of Anti-Semitism.* New York: Seabury, 1974.

Sandmel, S., *Anti-Semitism in the New Testament?* Philadelphia: Fortress, 1978.

———, *Philo's Place in Judaism: A Study of Conceptions of Abraham in Jewish Literature.* New York: KTAV, 1971.

C. Jesus

Banks, R., *Jesus and the Law in the Synoptic Tradition.* SNTSMS 28; Cambridge: University Press, 1975.

Barth, M., *Jesus the Jew,* trans. by F. Prussner. Atlanta: John Knox, 1978.

Berger, K., *Die Gesetzesauslegung Jesu: Ihr historischer Hintergrund im Judentum und im Alten Testament. Teil 1: Mar-*

kus und Parallelen. Neukirchen-Vluyn: Neukirchener, 1972.

Bultmann, R., *Jesus and the Word*, trans. by L. P. Smith and E. H. Lantero. New York: Scribner, 1934 (original publication 1929).

Bornkamm, G., *Jesus of Nazareth*, trans. by I. F. McLuskey with J. M. Robinson. New York: Harper and Row, 1960.

Falk, H., *Jesus the Pharisee: A New Look at the Jewishness of Jesus*. New York: Paulist, 1985.

Riches, J., *Jesus and the Transformation of Judaism*. New York: Seabury, 1982.

Sanders, E. P., *Jesus and Judaism*. Philadelphia: Fortress, 1985.

Tosato, A., "The Law of Leviticus 18:18: A Reexamination," *CBQ* 46 (1984) 199–214.

Vermes, G., *Jesus the Jew: A Historian's Reading of the Gospels*. New York: Macmillan, 1974.

Wild, R. A., "The Encounter between Pharisaic and Christian Judaism: Some Early Gospel Evidence," *NovT* 27 (1985) 105–24.

D. Early Church

Dahl, N. A., "The Crucified Messiah," *The Crucified Messiah and Other Essays*. (Minneapolis: Augsburg, 1974) 10–36 (original publication 1960).

Dunn, J. D. G., "Mark 2:1–3:6: a Bridge between Jesus and Paul on the Question of the Law," *NTS* 30 (1984) 395–415.

Heitmüller, W., "Hellenistic Christianity before Paul," *The Writings of St. Paul*, ed. by W. A. Meeks. (New York: Norton, 1972) 308–19 (original publication 1912).

Hengel, M., *Acts and the History of Earliest Christianity*, trans, by J. Bowden. Philadelphia: Fortress, 1980.

————, "Between Jesus and Paul: The 'Hellenists,' the 'Seven' and Stephen," *Between Jesus and Paul*, trans. by J. Bowden (Philadelphia: Fortress, 1983) 1–29.

————, "The Origins of the Christian Mission," ibid. 48–64.

Schmithals, W., *Paul and James*, trans. by D. M. Barton. SBT 46; Naperville, IL: Allenson, 1965.

Scholem, G., *Major Trends in Jewish Mysticism*. Jerusalem: Schocken, 1941.

Scroggs, R., "The Earliest Hellenistic Christianity," *Religions in Antiquity: Essays in Memory of Erwin Ramsdell Goodenough*, ed. by J. Neusner (Supplements to Numen 14; Leiden: Brill, 1968) 176–206.

E. Conservative Jewish Christianity

Bagatti, B., *The Church from the Circumcision: History and Archeology of the Judeo-Christians*, trans. by E. Hoarde. Publications of the Studium Biblicum Franciscanum, Smaller Series, 2; Jerusalem: Franciscan Printing Press, 1971.

Danielou, J., *A History of Early Christianity before the Council of Nicea. Vol 1: The Theology of Jewish Christianity*, trans, by J. A. Baker. Philadelphia: Westminster, 1964.

Judéo-Christianisme: Recherches historiques et theologiques offertes en hommage au Cardinal Jean Danielou. Recherches de Science Religieuse 60 (1972) 1–323.

Longenecker, R. N., *The Christology of Early Jewish Christianity*. SBT, second series, 17; Naperville, IL: Allenson, 1970.

Schoeps, H. J., *Jewish Christianity: Factional Disputes in the Early Church*, trans. by D. R. A. Hare. Philadelphia: Fortress, 1969.

———, *Theologie und Geschichte des Judenchristentums*. Tübingen: Mohr, 1949.

Schonfield, H. J., *The History of Jewish Christianity: From the First to the Twentieth Century*. London: Duckworth, 1936.

Strecker, G., "On the Problem of Jewish Christianity," in W. Bauer, *Orthodoxy and Heresy in Earliest Christianity*, trans. ed. by R. A. Kraft and G. Krodel (Philadelphia: Fortress, 1971) 241–85.

1. Jewish Rejection of Jewish Christianity

Katz, S., "Issues in the Separation of Judaism and Christianity after 70 CE: A Reconsideration," *JBL* 103 (1984) 43–76.

Kimmelman, R., "*Birkat Ha-Minim* and the Lack of Evidence for an Anti-Christian Jewish Prayer in Late Antiquity," *Jewish and Christian Self-Definition. Vol 2: Aspects of Judaism in the Greco-Roman Period*, ed. by E. P. Sanders with A. I. Baumgarten and A. Mendelson (Philadelphia: Fortress, 1981) 226–44.

Lerle, E., "Liturgische Reformen des Synagogengottesdienstes als Antwort auf die judenchristliche Mission des ersten Jahrhunderts," *NovT* 10 (1968) 31–42.

Schiffman, L., "At the Crossroads: Tannaitic Perspectives on the Jewish-Christian Schism," *Jewish and Christian Self-Definition. Vol 2*, 115–56.

———, *Who Was a Jew? Rabbinic and Halakhic Perspectives on the Jewish-Christian Schism*. Hoboken, NJ: KTAV, 1985.

Segal, A., *Two Powers in Heaven: Early Rabbinic Reports about Christianity and Gnosticism.* Studies in Judaism and Late Antiquity 25; Leiden: Brill, 1977.

2. Gospel of Matthew

Barth, G., "Matthew's Understanding of the Law," in G. Bornkamm, G. Barth, H. J. Held, *Tradition and Interpretation in Matthew,* trans. by P. Scott (Philadelphia: Westminster, 1963) 58–164.
Carlston, C., "The Things that Defile (Mark 7:14) and the Law in Matthew and Mark," *NTS* 15 (1968–9) 75–96.
Davies, W. D., *The Setting of the Sermon on the Mount.* Cambridge: University Press, 1964.
Hare, D. R. A., *The Theme of Jewish Persecution of Christians in the Gospel according to St. Matthew.* SNTSMS 6; Cambridge: University Press, 1967.

3. Gospel of John

Brown, R. E., *The Community of the Beloved Disciple.* New York/Ramsey: Paulist, 1979.
Martyn, J. L., *The Gospel of John in Christian History: Essays for Interpreters.* New York/Ramsey: Paulist, 1979.
———, *History and Theology in the Fourth Gospel.* New York: Harper and Row, 1968.
Meeks, W. A., " 'Am I a Jew?'—Johannine Christianity and Judaism," *Judaism, Christianity and Other Greco-Roman Cults,* ed. by J. Neusner (Leiden: Brill, 1975) 1.163–86.
Pancaro, S., *The Law in the Fourth Gospel: The Torah and the Gospel, Moses and Jesus, Judaism and Christianity according to John.* NovT Sup 42; Leiden: Brill, 1975.
———, " 'People of God' in St. John's Gospel," *NTS* 16 (1969–70) 114–29.

Townsend, J. T., "The Gospel of John and the Jews: The Story of a Religious Divorce," *Anti-Semitism and the Foundations of Christianity*, 72–97. (See B)

4. Elkasaites, Ebionites, Cerinthians

Klijn, A. J. F. and G. J. Reinink, *Patristic Evidence for Jewish-Christian Sects*. NovT Sup 36; Leiden: Brill, 1973.

5. Clementine Homilies and Recognitions

Schoeps, H. J., *Jewish Christianity*. (See E)
———, *Theologie und Geschichte des Judenchristentums*. (See E)
Strecker, G., *Das Judenchristentum in den Pseudoclementinen*. Berlin: Akademie, 1958.

6. Ephemeral Conservative Jewish Christianity

Barrett, C. K., "Jews and Judaizers in the Epistles of Ignatius," *Jews, Greeks and Christians: Religious Cultures in Late Antiquity*, ed. by R. Hammerton-Kelly and R. Scroggs. (Leiden: Brill, 1976) 220–44.
Donahue, P., "Jewish Christianity in the Letters of Ignatius of Antioch," *VC* 32 (1978) 81–93.
de Lange, N., *Origen and the Jews: Studies in Jewish-Christian Relations in Third-century Palestine*. Cambridge: University Press, 1976.
Wilken, R. L., *John Chrysostom and the Jews: Rhetoric and Reality in the Late Fourth Century*. Transformation of the Classical Heritage 4; Berkeley, Los Angeles and London: University of California Press, 1983.
———, *Judaism and the Early Christian Mind: A Study of Cyril of Alexandria's Exegesis and Theology*. New Haven: Yale, 1971.

F. Liberal Jewish Christianity

Jervell, J., *The Unknown Paul: Essays on Luke–Acts and Early Christian History*. Minneapolis: Augsburg, 1984.

1. Paul

Barth, M., *The People of God*. Journal for the Study of the New Testament Supplement Series 5; Sheffield: JSOT Press, 1983.

Callan, T., "Pauline Midrash: The Exegetical Background of Gal 3:19b," *JBL* 99 (1980) 549–67.

Dahl, N. A., "Contradictions in Scripture," *Studies in Paul* (Minneapolis: Augsburg, 1978) 159–77.

Davies, W. D., *Paul and Rabbinic Judaism: Some Rabbinic Elements in Pauline Theology*. London: SPCK, 1958.

Gaston, L., "Paul and the Torah," *Anti-Semitism and the Foundations of Christianity*, 48–71. (See B)

Sanders, E. P., *Paul, the Law, and the Jewish People*. Philadelphia: Fortress, 1983.

Stendahl, K., *Paul Among Jews and Gentiles and Other Essays*. Philadelphia: Fortress, 1976.

2. Luke-Acts

Jervell, J., *Luke and the People of God*. Minneapolis: Augsburg, 1972.

Tiede, D. L., *Prophecy and History in Luke-Acts*. Philadelphia: Fortress, 1980.

3. Nazoraeans

Klijn, A. J. F., "Jerome's Quotations from a Nazoraean Interpretation of Isaiah," *Judéo-Christianisme*, 241–55. (See E)

Klijn, A. J. F. and G. Reinink, *Patristic Evidence for Jewish-Christian Sects.* (See E–4).

4. *Decline of Liberal Jewish Christianity*

Brandon, S. G. F., *The Fall of Jerusalem and the Christian Church: A Study of the Effects of the Jewish Overthrow of AD 70 on Christianity.* London: SPCK, 1968.

Donfried, K. P., *The Romans Debate.* Minneapolis: Augsburg, 1977.

Lüdemann, G., "The Successors of Pre-70 Jerusalem Christianity: A Critical Evaluation of the Pella Tradition," *Jewish and Christian Self-Definition. Vol 1: The Shaping of Christianity in the Second and Third Centuries,* ed. by E. P. Sanders. (Philadelphia: Fortress, 1980) 161–73.

Simon, M., "La migration à Pella. Legende ou realite?" *Judéo-Christianisme,* 37–54. (See E)

G. Liberal Gentile Christianity

1. *Jewish Arguments*

Connolly, R. H., *Didascalia Apostolorum: The Syriac Version Translated and Accompanied by the Verona Latin Fragments.* Oxford: Clarendon Press, 1929.

Neusner, J., *Aphrahat and Judaism: The Christian-Jewish Argument in Fourth Century Iran.* Studies Post-Biblica 19; Leiden: Brill, 1971.

Ruether, R. R., *Faith and Fratricide.* (See B)

Stylianopolis, T., *Justin Martyr and the Mosaic Law.* SBLDS 20; Missoula, MT: Scholars, 1975.

Williams, A. Lukyn, *Adversus Judaeos. A Bird's Eye View of Christian Apologiae until the Renaissance.* Cambridge: University Press, 1935.

2. Marcion and the Gnostics

Blackman, E. C., *Marcion and His Influence*. London: SPCK, 1948.

Efroymson, D. P., "The Patristic Connection," *Anti-Semitism and the Foundations of Christianity*, 98–117. (See B).

Harnack, A. von, *Marcion: Das Evangelium vom fremden Gott*. Leipzig: Hinrichs, 1924.

Hoffmann, R. J., *Marcion: On the Restitution of Christianity. An Essay on the Development of Radical Paulinist Theology in the Second Century*. AAR Academy Series 46; Chico, CA: Scholars, 1984.

Jonas, H., *The Gnostic Religion*. Boston: Beacon, 1962.

3. Pagan Criticism of Christianity

Barnes, T. D., *Constantine and Eusebius*. Cambridge: Harvard, 1981.

Benko, S., *Pagan Rome and the Early Christians*. Bloomington: Indiana University Press, 1984.

Bowersock, G. W., *Julian the Apostate*. Cambridge: Harvard, 1978.

Efroymson, D. P., "The Patristic Connection." (See G–2).

Wilken, R. L., *The Christians as the Romans Saw Them*. New Haven: Yale, 1984.

INDEX OF REFERENCES

A. Biblical References

B. Jewish Literature

C. Christian Literature

D. Greek and Latin Literature

E. Modern Authors